Contents

Coaching Up and Down the Generations

Lisa Haneberg

ASTD PRESS

Alexandria, Virginia

BK

Berrett–Koehler Publishers, Inc.
San Francisco
a BK Business book

ASTD Press is an internationally renowned source of insightful and practical information on workplace learning and performance topics, including training basics, evaluation and return-on-investment, instructional systems development, e-learning, leadership, and career development.

Ordering information: Books published by ASTD Press can be purchased by visiting ASTD's website at store.astd.org or by calling 800.628.2783 or 703.683.8100.

Library of Congress Control Number: 2009937673

ISBN-10: 1-56286-719-9
ISBN-13: 978-1-56286-719-5

ASTD Press Editorial Staff:
Director: Adam Chesler
Manager, ASTD Press: Jacqueline Edlund-Braun
Project Manager, Content Acquisition: Justin Brusino
Senior Associate Editor: Tora Estep
Associate Editor: Victoria DeVaux
Editorial Assistant: Stephanie Castellano

Copyeditor: Alfred Imhoff
Indexer: April Michelle Davis
Proofreader: Kris Patenaude
Interior Design and Production: Kathleen Schaner
Cover Design: Ana Ilieva Foreman

Printed by Versa Press Inc., East Peoria, IL, www.versapress.com

Acknowledgments

My approaches to coaching have changed a lot over the years, and I have learned important distinctions and skills from many people. I am thankful for all the coaches who allowed me to pull them into great conversations. I am also grateful to the folks who participated in the coaching survey I did for this book and who inspired the stories that I hope will now inspire you, the reader. Thanks to the wonderful folks at ASTD Press for supporting this project, and particularly its nontraditional vibe and direction. I value our partnership a great deal. Thanks to Berrett-Koehler Publishers for its interest in this book and for signing on as copublisher; I am honored to be a part of its author team. Thanks to Cleve Callison for helping me research parts of the book. And last but not least, I would like to thank my husband, Bill, for making it easier and acceptable for me to neglect home chores so that I could write this book!

Introduction

Beyond the Clichés and Worn-Out Talk About Generations

This book is for professionals who want to better catalyze success at many levels of the organization and with colleagues of all ages, persuasions, and hair color. Why did I write it? Let me share with you two uncommon beliefs upon which this book is built:

- The first belief has to do with the essence of coaching.
- The second belief pertains to the challenge of coaching and being coached by people of different ages and experience levels.

I explain these two beliefs just below. But first, a few words of background. Search the Internet and you will find thousands of books, classes, and articles offering suggestions about how to coach people. There are coaching forms, 12-step programs, assessments, surveys, and 360-degree feedback processes. Some of these resources recommend a structured regimen featuring templates for conducting typical coaching conversations. These resources offer valuable information, and most of what I have seen has been technically correct.

So what's the problem? My concern is that many "how to coach" resources are far too prescriptive and miss addressing what I think are the most important aspects of coaching. Great coaching cannot and should not be defined as a set of practices or as a competency.

Author's Aside

If coaching was expressed as a competency, it would have to be called "When asked, help performers with whatever they are up to using whatever means will be most helpful to them and then embrace that you might never know what you did that helped, or if you helped, or when the help became helpful." I don't see that description being put into a competency model, do you? How about "agile, service-oriented persistence with a tolerance for the unexplainable and a willingness to go down a path that is not yours, does not interest you, and requires that you buy new shoes to traverse unharmed"?

The essence of coaching is responding to someone who wants coaching in a way that most helps her now or in the future. I define coaching as a developmental conversation *as assessed and requested by the performer*. (As you may have noticed, I am using the terms *coach* and *performer*. I hate the terms *protégé, mentee,* and *coachee* because they seem old fashioned and hark back to a time when wisdom came down from on high. *Performer* is not perfect either, but it puts the focus where it ought to be— away from the coach and onto the person with the goal.)

We do not get to say if we are great coaches, and we should not try to call the shots by setting the agenda for each conversation. In fact, coaching is better when we have less control over the conversation. Coaching and control do not blend well at all. (If you, like me, are a recovering control freak, this notion might not sit well with you. Alas, it is true—we really are not in control, and less in control the harder we try to seem so. Join me in recovery, and swim in egalitarian—dare I say service-oriented— waters, letting the tides and currents move you about. You will find it a liberating experience!)

Learning does not ooze from filled-in forms or plop out at the end of any process or regimen. In the 20 years that I have been coaching professionals, I have continued to be surprised to learn what I have done that has made the greatest difference for each individual with whom I have worked. Sometimes I never learn what worked, but I see that she is zooming forward and rejoice in that.

This is my belief about coaching, and I invite you to explore it with me here in this book. You might think that this description will have made it difficult to write about how to coach well, and this is true. I pulled out a few hairs, added more gray ones, and twisted my head around entirely a few times while determining how to be concrete about an ambiguous and seemingly magical topic. It was fun!

Generational Considerations

As you likely surmised from the title, this is a book that merges an exploration of what it takes to be a great coach with how to better connect and communicate with professionals of all ages. Like the topic of coaching, there has been a lot of literature written about the tendencies of the four generations: the Traditionalists, the Baby Boomers, Generation X, and Generation Y or the Millennials. During the last five years, every business conference I have attended has featured presentations on the topic of generational differences. The media has picked up on this, and the phrase "four generations in the workplace" returns more than 80,000 hits when entered in a Google search. (It's to a point where the most common answer to questions exploring why it is hard to improve our organizations is "Well, we are dealing with four generations in the workplace.")

As I approached the writing of this book, I had a bit of a personal dilemma because the multigenerational topic seems overexposed. One anecdotal bit of evidence of this is that I was asked by two different program chairs for conferences at which I will be speaking to *not* talk about generational issues. Apparently, we're tired of the topic!

And yet—and yet, we are not connecting and communicating and helping each other learn like we ought to. We all need to help interested professionals get better, move forward, and obliterate barriers. We should help experienced professionals stay relevant. We should create change-ready organizations in which agility is as common as breathing and changes are received with the same kind of delight we see in people's eyes when there's free pepperoni pizza in the conference room.

(This reference might be culturally aimed at North America. Substitute your country's favorite irresistible, nutritionless junk food. That said, the psychoactive effects of the chemicals found in cheap grocery store pepperoni make it quite a unique pleasure.)

If you are young, you have much to share and learn. If you are older, you have much to share and learn. And we know that to be a great coach, you might not have to know anything about any particular topic except how to be helpful—anyone can coach anyone, if the conditions are right.

We might be sick of hearing about the four generations in the workplace, but this is not because we have figured it all out. And maybe that is the wrong goal anyway—I don't think we can or should try to figure each other out. The solution to our lack of understanding, communication, relationships, and collaboration is not reading a book about the four generations or attending a diversity class about them or sitting through a conference speech about them. I think that for us to better work with—affect, communicate with, reach, and influence—people of all ages, we need to change our goals for communication and coaching and change how we define success and our work responsibilities. The approach I recommend is personal and internal, and it will thus require us to give up a few beliefs and replace them with more helpful notions about how we can best contribute to each other and our organizations.

How do we help people who think in ways that are fundamentally different from ours? How will our communication and listening make it through each other's filters and preferences? And more practically, how can we help someone who uses tools and jargon that seem to come from another planet? (This goes both ways, too. We Baby-Boomerasauruses cling to some pretty weird tools, like Skinnerian reinforcement systems, hand-drawn process maps, staff meetings, and $800 industrial training films.)

Oh, what fun we will have exploring these enigmatic qualities of workplace human relationships and effectiveness! I hope this book is a catalyst for you, and I invite you to jump into the coming pages open to the possibility that they could be game changers for you—as a coach and as a performer.

The Phrase "Up and Down the Generations"

As I've suggested above and you will read in the chapters that follow, I want to encourage coaching and relationship building between professionals of all ages. I would like to see 60-year-olds become raving fans of 25-year-olds and 35-year-olds find the time they spend with the 50-year-olds precious and illuminating. I'd like the new college recruit to see how cool the 55-year-old is, and I want the 45-year-old to jump in and love—feeling alive like she has not been for years—being coached by the 21-year-old whiz kid and technology savant. When I write the phrase "up and down the generations," this is the vision I am sharing. It is not just that each generation learns from each other, but also that there is an electricity present due to the coming together of so many great yet various hearts and minds.

With four generations—Traditionalists, Baby Boomers, Generation X, and Generation Y or Millennials—working side by side in our increasingly global workplaces, the key processes of transferring knowledge, developing teams, and collaborating have become a bigger challenge. To help organizations build strong coaching and mentoring practices, I created a coaching model and program aimed at helping all employees better learn from each other. This Coaching Up and Down the Generations Network Model of Coaching (see figure 1) stresses how important it is for professionals at all levels, of all ages, and from all backgrounds to connect, collaborate, and learn with and from each other. The coaching program that uses this model addresses the barriers individuals face when they coach, and are coached by, others—especially the challenges related to influencing people who have different beliefs, work preferences, and communication habits. Throughout this book, the specific topics that I explore reflect this model.

A Note on the "He or She" Problem

In each of my books, I have had to decide how to handle the he/she/they issue. Do I write in the plural most of the time—referring to "they" as much as possible? Or do I write "he or she," "him or her," and "his or hers"

Figure I-1. The Coaching Up and Down the Generations Network Model of Coaching

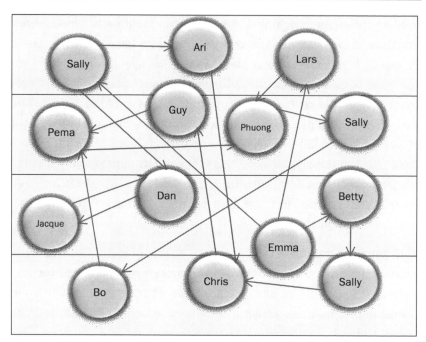

Network Coaching: Learning should occur in all directions

Source: MPI Consulting (www.managementperformance.com); used with permission.

a million times? In the old days, it was acceptable to simply use "he" and so on. In this book, I have decided to use "she," "her," and "hers" when writing generically about an individual. Why? Because I'm a chick, and I think readers know that the examples apply to all readers. Sticking to one gender helps you, the reader, to easily move through paragraphs, allowing you to focus on their meaning.

What's Next

In the six chapters that follow, you will find two kinds of practical information—information about what constitutes great coaching, and information about how to get to know each of the four generations in the workplace. You will also learn how to develop strategies for bringing these two subsets of information together so that you can catalyze more coaching up and down the generations. Here's a rundown of each chapter's focus:

- Chapter 1 clarifies what great coaching is and is not, what it looks like in action, and the impact that coaching ought to have on performers.
- Chapter 2 peeks inside the lives and motivations of the four generations—the Traditionalists, Baby Boomers, Generation X, and Millennials—so that you can better appreciate and form partnerships with your diverse coworkers.
- Chapter 3 explores the coaching best practices and skills that can help both coaches and performers learn from each other.
- Chapter 4 challenges all readers and performers to improve their effectiveness by becoming more coachable and shares techniques that coaches can use to improve performer coachability.
- Chapter 5 shows how coaches and performers can form partnerships to catalyze breakthroughs and to improve the speed and energy of their progress.
- Chapter 6 outlines several important considerations for creating a work environment where coaching up and down the generations can prosper.

Chapter 1

Coaching for Catalysts

Fundamentals for Creating Great Coaching Moments

When thinking about what distinguishes great from poor coaching, I remember a conversation I overheard early in my career. I was 20 years old, with an ego that outpaced my accomplishments by a long shot (in other words, I was a normal 20-year-old). I am going to call the performer Jack and the coach Jill. Jack was the controller, and Jill was the front desk manager in the large hotel where we all worked. I was the assistant food and beverage director. Jack wanted to implement a new system for purchase orders, but his ideas were not being received well by the other managers. Jack asked Jill to listen to the plan and help brainstorm ways to make the plan better for all involved. At first, Jill seemed reluctant to comment or criticize, but then she started asking great questions that led Jack to reflect on and share the reasons the other managers had concerns. Jill had her own opinions, but what Jack needed was someone to help him see what he already knew, which was that his plan would not succeed unless he became more flexible and accommodating.

I can remember thinking that if Jack would have asked me for advice, I would have jumped right in and told him what needed to be changed and why—which was not what he needed. Jack asked for and was responsive to Jill's thoughts and questions. Jill resisted giving advice and listened well.

After the coaching conversation, Jack was highly motivated to change his purchase order proposal, and the new plan was well received by the management team. The coaching conversation was brief and effective—yet it was intimate, deep, and provocative.

Author's Aside

Resisting the urge to control people and situations is a huge challenge for coaches and managers. It is most important when coaching and collaborating with others, because success depends on the performer owning her process and results.

Jill used three of the four distinctions that I have selected to describe in this chapter. These distinctions can make a significant difference toward helping you help others. In the pages that follow, I also offer five coaching killers that can reduce your efficacy. But before we dive into the specifics, let's step back and look at the big picture: What's the purpose of coaching? And to begin, let's consider an even more fundamental question: What is coaching?

What Is Coaching?

Coaching is a service that we have the opportunity to provide when performers seek our assistance. It occurs as a conversation that could be done in person, over the phone, in writing, or through other connections. The service of coaching might look like many things, depending on the varying needs and requests of the performer. Sometimes coaching feels like being a scout on a nature expedition—where we are asked to share what we see, hear, and think about something from our vantage point. Coaching might also look and feel like attending a concert, where our main role is to listen and let the performers share their interpretations. Very often, the work of a coach is that of a puzzle master—with our job being to notice the pieces, make observations, and ask questions that help performers bring together their vision, goals, and ways forward.

I just reread the previous paragraph and realize that you might find it frustratingly vague. I don't mean to be obtuse and abstract, but coaching is not a cut-and-dried thing that looks the same every time. Think about the last time when you received great coaching, and reflect on how the conversation started, unfolded, and ended. I would bet that the moment you are recalling was not scheduled in Microsoft Outlook and was not part of a defined and structured coaching conversation.

Author's Aside

I do schedule coaching appointments, by the way. I am not saying that regular coaching relationships are not valid or helpful. My point here is that I think breakthroughs happen because of the quality of the moment and that this is not something that can be planned into an agenda—it must come through deep listening and connection. And even though I might suggest planning questions and "homework" for my coaching clients, I do this not because I think these specific actions are what great coaching is about. The assignments are ways into a conversation that must then take on a life of its own to be of any use.

Like snowflakes, every coaching moment is unique. Here's the bottom-line definition: Coaching is a developmental conversation requested, welcomed, and driven by the performer that enables her to better achieve her goals.

What Is the Purpose of Coaching?

On the basis of my definition of coaching, its purpose should be clear—coaching needs to help the performer move forward in some small or big way. Great coaching fuels performers with inspiration, new ideas, clarity, shortcuts, focus, knowledge, or some combination of these types of progress.

Coaching is very cool work, and I cannot think of a better way to spend time with a fellow professional. I get a rush of satisfaction when something I say or do enables a performer to zoom toward her goal with velocity (by velocity, I mean speed and direction; when people move toward goals with velocity, they progress with an oomph that is wonderful and that imbues their work with energy). Think about the last time you catalyzed a breakthrough—wasn't that fun? And it is a privilege to be able to have an impact on others at work. If I look back on the previous month, one of my most memorable moments was hearing from a coaching client who said she felt amazing, on the right track, and confident. During our first coaching session, she reported feeling like a failure, stressed, and unable to figure out what to do differently. Something wonderful happened in a very short period of time to change her performance trajectory, and I feel honored that she invited me into the conversation to participate and help. Being there for her—whatever that meant—was my purpose as her coach, and this is the purpose of all coaching: to be there to help.

Four Distinguishing Characteristics of Great Coaching

With these definitions in mind, let's explore a few fundamentals that tap into the art and science of coaching—with a nod to chaos theory. These distinctions can help you create productive conversations with performers:

- pull-versus-push coaching
- coaches as catalysts
- the coach's sponge stance
- accountability and structure.

Author's Aside

Human systems share some of the characteristics of chaotic systems. In chaotic systems, like the weather, the outcome cannot be predicted, and there is a sensitivity to initial conditions—meaning that current conditions are affected by an earlier condition that is not known or fully understood. Thus, coaching conversations can be directionally correct, well intended, and logical, but because they are part of human systems, they still may not produce the results we predict.

Pull-versus-Push Coaching

I was talking with the very smart Jeffrey Ford on the phone last week, and he offered this simple and elegant thought about coaching: "There is no coaching without a request." I love the way he phrased this, and I think he's correct. Let's break his thought down a bit, because I think there's a lot of confusion out there about the type of conversations that lead to good coaching. A request is a way of pulling the coach into a conversation. But then why do so many of the conversations we call coaching begin with a push instead of a pull?

Author's Aside

Jeffrey Ford has been a professor of management for many years at Ohio State University, and with his wife, Laurie Ford, has coauthored a great book, *The Four Conversations* (Ford and Ford 2009; also see www.professorford .com).

The short answer is that many of these "push" conversations are simply not really coaching. Let me give a few examples. I frequently receive requests to help train managers to be better coaches. My client uses the term "coaching," but she actually wants me to help her managers counsel employees who are not meeting expectations. That's something managers need to do, but it is not really coaching. File this skill under *performance counseling.*

And then I have worked with managers and leaders who believed that coaching was an opportunity to share their sageness—to share their lessons learned, to share ideas and give advice to less experienced professionals. This is very important to do, too, but this is not really coaching either. File this skill under *teaching and advice giving.*

I get calls from executives who are worried about one of their managers who they fear "might not make it." (Translation: The manager is on the verge of being fired or demoted. Why didn't they call earlier? Why did they wait until the manager is heading over a steep cliff to ask for help?

And why don't managers see where their career is headed and seek help? But that's a topic for another book.) Something she is doing is bad enough that it could affect her career, and coaching is being offered as a last ditch effort to save her job. These fix-it situations sometimes involve coaching, but often what really needs to be done is a combination of diagnosis, feedback, direction, and tough love accountability. Things should not come to this, but they sometimes do. And although coaches are often hired to help, I don't think of this as coaching (it is really more like being a somewhat detached boss figure). File this skill under *individualized leadership planning and feedback.*

These three types of well-intended help are pushed onto the performer. Managers push all kinds of things on a daily basis—the vast majority with good intent and to good results. But this is not coaching.

I recently conducted a survey about coaching preferences, and the most frequent and vivid message offered by the participants was that they want us to pull, not push, coaching. They said:

- "Don't force it."
- "Help me when I want the help."
- "Take the time to learn about my goals."
- "Stop pontificating."
- "Don't get angry if I don't take your advice—it's just your advice."
- "Encourage me."

This is just a sampling of the many comments I received along these lines. These results did not differ by age group, by the way—this was a theme for all generations. No one wants to be pushed! And yet—and yet most of us spend much more time pushing what we think is coaching instead of pulling what others will regard as coaching. We do mean well. It takes time and care to provide pull coaching, because it requires that we ask more questions, be more flexible, recognize and respect the other person's coachability triggers (see chapter 4 for more on coachability), and get to know her and her goals. It is easier to project what we think is best for our employees onto them wrapped in a candy-coated pill called coaching.

Here's one way to increase your opportunities for providing pull coaching: Take the initiative to get to know your colleagues. Understand what they want to achieve and how they want to contribute to the organization. Allow yourself to be inspired by their interests and engagement. (If they don't seem engaged and interested, keep listening and keep learning about what's important to them; they are engaged and interested in something.) Get to know each person in ways that work for her—methods, timing, level of formality, frequency. My survey participants also said that they did not want people interrupting them with an offer of coaching when they are very busy, near a deadline, or in the zone doing something else.

Pull coaching is a service, and it will be best delivered when we adopt a service mentality. How we serve, what we serve, and when we serve it should be defined—and requested—by the customer.

One habit that I find leads to pull coaching opportunities begins during the moments after a meeting ends, using what I call an after-the-buzzer three-point question. Here's how it works. As the meeting is wrapping up and people are beginning to collect their papers and call dibs on any remaining donuts, I ask someone an open-ended question about something she is working on. Often, she will have expressed some concern over her progress during the meeting. The question is respectful and shows my genuine curiosity. Here are a couple of examples:

- Sally, I found your report interesting. How did you discover that the numbers weren't matching up?
- Sally, you have your work cut out, don't you? Do you have enough help from people who can help you dig into the analysis?

And sometimes I use a three-point offer, like "Sally, I have struggled with vendor delays too, and would be happy to grab a latte to swap stories and ideas if that is ever of interest." If the performer wants to engage in a follow-up conversation, she will contact me. A committed performer is likely to see the opportunity and pull me in for a coaching conversation. Many fruitful coaching experiences have started with an after-the-buzzer three-point question.

But what if no one pulls you into a coaching conversation? What does that mean? There are several reasons why you might not be seeing many opportunities to provide pull coaching:

- Performers don't think of you as approachable.
- Performers don't think you are interested in coaching.
- You tend to take over conversations.
- Performers don't know you well enough to feel comfortable seeking your help.
- Some performers lack the confidence needed to request coaching.
- You come across as judgmental or not welcoming.

If you want to be an effective coach and be pulled into more coaching conversations, you need to be someone with whom people want to talk. Show your interest in your colleagues' goals, and express an open curiosity for how others work. Be likable, and resist the need to control conversations. Take note of your conversations, and consider whether you spend more time pushing or being pulled into coaching.

Coaches as Catalysts

You are striding through the woods down a rocky, unpaved, and meandering footpath. Rain has made the trail muddy, and a whipping wind is uprooting saplings and cracking off branches that are falling in your way. The sun peeks through the green canopy on occasion. As you walk, hike, jog, or slog—your speed changes with the conditions—you cycle through feelings of optimism, success, stuckness, and weariness. The path seems longer than you had imagined, and you wonder if you will make it to your destination.

Then something happens that speeds you forward. You discover a shortcut. Someone helps you over the boulder. You find the perfect hiking stick. The sunlight leads you to an open patch where you can adjust your bearings. The fog lifts, and the way is clear. Something happens that makes your journey easier—you experience a catalyst.

This is a book about how we can help each other reach our destinations. The path represents our goals. The boulders, branches, weather, and bends in the road represent all the barriers and challenges we face. The catalysts (see the sidebar) generally come from some kind of coaching or learning experience. Be a catalyst!

> ### *Catalyst:* cat·a·lyst
>
> 1. A substance that accelerates a chemical reaction without itself undergoing change.
> 2. Somebody who stimulates change or speeds up a result.
> 3. A tool that makes a task easier.

Great coaching catalyzes lightbulb—or "aha!"—moments. Strictly speaking, a catalyst is a substance that increases the rate of a chemical reaction. Although they participate in reactions, catalysts are neither consumed by nor incorporated into the products of the reactions. There is just as much catalyst at the end of the reaction as there was at the beginning. In most cases, only small amounts of catalysts are needed to increase reaction rates.

Catalysts work by providing easier ways for reactions to occur. A good analogy is a bridge over a valley. Without the bridge, it might be possible to cross the valley by driving down one twisting road and then back up another. But the bridge allows the valley to be crossed more quickly and with less energy. It does not reduce the amount of energy needed to drive down one side and up the other, but instead it offers an alternate way to achieve the same results while using less energy.

People can be catalysts, too. You have likely served as a catalyst for someone this week. Great coaches are, above all else, catalysts—they help people scoot forward by making things easier. A jolt of inspiration or clarity propels them into action, conversation, or further examination and fuels their efforts.

How can we learn to be catalysts? How can we develop more catalytic conversational skills? I have studied and written about the nature of breakthroughs and catalysts, and have found four simple ways for coaches to become better catalysts:

- Be curious.
- Be proactive.
- Be observant.
- Be courageous.

Be Curious

The more you encourage your natural curiosity, the more likely that you will be able to catalyze transformation. I see a strong connection between curiosity, coaching, and learning because learning happens in layers. The outer layer is the surface, and that's the kind of learning that occurs in many training sessions. As we go deeper, learning becomes much more personal and connective—connecting to work, interests, problems, and passions. Curiosity is one vehicle we can use to go deeper. We keep hiking because we are curious about what's around the next bend. We keep listening because we are curious about where the conversation is heading. We ask more questions because we are curious about how the performer will respond. Let your curiosity flourish. Ask open-ended questions about what things mean and how they operate. Take an interest in understanding why and how things work. Your questions—your curiosity—might open up a whole new way of thinking or approach for the performer.

Be Proactive

It's tough to be a catalyst if you are not proactive. Listen and respond to what performers are saying—and to what they obviously are *not* saying. Challenge the performer by stepping the conversation up to the next level of intimacy, complexity, or controversy. Take the initiative to offer uncommon interpretations of the situation. Don't take months to offer your support—the performer might need you today! Take the initiative to put the right people together in a conversation. Do whatever it takes to be responsive and helpful.

Be Observant

I have known too many professionals who failed to see what was happening in their immediate work environment—they were not observant. To be a great catalyst, you have to notice what's going on. Keep up with current events, trends, and feelings by being in the company of others—eat lunch in the break room, participate in informal conversations, get to meetings a few minutes early to get in on the pre-meeting chatter, and invite your peers to regular informal discussions over lattes down at the corner coffee shop. Notice the topics and behaviors (and perhaps people) that tend to engage or disengage meeting participants. Notice the major obstacles within the organization, and offer to help obliterate them. Share your observations in ways that stimulate the performer's input and interest—that create a pull situation.

Be Courageous

This next way of being a catalyst is the one I see the least. Great coaches are courageous people—they have to be, because that's how we make the greatest difference. Courage plays a big part in creating great dialogue because it's often what's not being said that needs to be said. Do you let discussions ride on the surface, or do you ask that one question—the tough question—that will turn the conversation upside down and get the performer nervously engaged? Having courage is not really risky; but you might find it uncomfortable or scary. Tension is not always a bad thing—it means that we are thinking and feeling.

Very small amounts of these behaviors can speed the progress of your conversations with performers. Be a catalyst today and make something happen. For more ways to help performers (or yourself) generate breakthroughs, see chapter 5, "Extra Credit: The Science of Breakthroughs."

● ● ●

Catalyst Haiku

My observations
Caused quite a ruckus today
Exhilarating!

● ● ●

The Coach's Sponge Stance

I have struggled to be a better listener most of my career. I have been, and probably sometimes still am, one of those irritating people who is obviously not listening. I have a tendency to interrupt people and catch myself thinking about what I am going to say next when others are talking. This is very bad behavior! And it is very common. For coaches, poor listening skills are deadly—like a quarterback who can't throw the football. It is for the listening-challenged out there, like myself, that I created the notion of the "sponge stance."

At one point in my career, I was doing 25 back-to-back training classes in a large office building in downtown Seattle. Each morning, I would enjoy a latte in the lobby Starbucks. These early moments were peaceful and reflective. I watched people line up for their caffeine fixes and sit at the small, round tables with colleagues and friends. I observed a large spectrum of listening styles and was most fascinated by the people who seemed completely engrossed in what the other person was saying. On the basis of this observation, I started concluding my management training sessions with the following imagery and invitation:

> Imagine that after this class you go down to the lobby Starbucks for a final infusion of caffeine. You are standing in line, and you notice that the person standing in front of you is someone you admire—someone famous, a great leader, author, innovator, or a historical figure. You summon the courage to introduce yourself to this person and ask her if she would like to have a coffee and chat with you. She agrees. Now imagine that you are sitting across from her at one of those small, round café tables. She is talking, and you are hanging on every word she is saying. Your eyes are fixed on her face, and you are unaware of what's going on beyond your conversation. You think she is amazing, and you are enjoying taking in each word, inflection, and nonverbal cue. You are like a sponge, fully soaking up her messages.
>
> Now imagine that you are in a meeting with one of your co-workers. She is amazing, too—everyone is amazing in some

way. What if you listened to your coworker with the same level of interest and focus that you gave the object of your admiration down at the Starbucks? What would that feel like for her? For you? Can you imagine being listened to in this way? Would you respond differently—more candidly, fully, deeply—if you felt like the other person cared to listen well?

This is the sponge stance—the way we listen when we demonstrate a complete interest in and focus on the other person. It's the way we listen when we think the other person is amazing—when we admire who she is and what she is doing. In the years that I have been telling people about the sponge stance, several have asked if what I am describing is the same thing as active listening (which means not interrupting, asking for clarification, not thinking about what you are going to say, parroting back what you hear, paying attention, empathizing, minimizing distractions, and reflecting on and synthesizing the information). I don't think the two approaches are the same—nor are they in conflict with one another. The sponge stance is listening that demonstrates our regard for the performer and our admiration for what she is trying to accomplish. Do you really hear what others are saying? If we want to help make big things happen, we need to listen deeply and well.

Accountability and Structure

I have a friend who needs to have structure in place to help her stay focused. If she promises to get X done by next Friday, she is more likely to do it—even if she made the promise to me (someone who would let her break her promise). My husband and I run or walk marathon and half-marathon races. Our training is much more focused if we are signed up for a race in the coming months. The structure and accountability is self-imposed—we could easily not show up for the race and no one would care—but it is still powerful.

In a pull system of coaching, coaches can help define accountability and structure, but the performers themselves must choose which particular measures and commitments will best help them stay focused and in action.

To help performers without pushing something onto them, ask questions that facilitate a collaborative discovery of potential accountability tools. Here are a few examples:

- Sally, I do my best work when I have a deadline. If this is true for you, too, is there a deadline or commitment to which you could agree that would help keep you on track?
- Many people find that they are more proactive when they frequently measure their progress. Are there measures or reports that would help you chart your progress?
- Adding some structure or accountability can be helpful to keep you focused and on track. What might be most helpful to you? Are you most motivated by deadlines, data, regular check-ins, promises to share the finished product, or some other form of commitment?

Structure and accountability enable performers to focus. By helping them discover the commitments that best serve their needs and style, we enable progress while retaining an environment of pull coaching.

It is also important that we help performers recover from commitment failures. What if the promise goes unmet? Few things can derail a performer's progress faster than self-doubt and feelings of failure. I can remember a time when I was caught in a downward spiral of self-doubt because it was clear to me that I was not going to be able to meet my self-imposed measure of success. My friend had to suggest—three times, with three different approaches—that I allow myself to have a "plan B." At first, I was stubborn and would not accept the possibility of an alternative commitment and definition of success. Ultimately, however, I created a plan B and was able to continue forward. As coaches, we should help people slowed by a failure or setback discover and define their plan B.

Building on the Four Distinctions

Great coaches are pulled into conversations, catalyze progress, listen well, and provide the structure and accountability that the performer seeks. When you seek coaching, this is what you want, right? These four distinctions are the foundation of great coaching. There are many other coaching skills that you can develop and might find helpful, but these are the most important for creating a conversation and environment that is most helpful to the performer.

Five Coaching Killers

Too often, well-meaning coaches inadvertently do the wrong things and are not helpful. Like doctors taking the Hippocratic Oath, I think coaches should hold themselves to the standard of never doing harm.

Author's Aside

I have written about catalysts on my Management Craft blog (www .managementcraft.com) and in my book *Two Weeks to a Breakthrough: How to Zoom toward Your Goal in 14 Days or Less* (Haneberg 2007).

And yet we all have made things worse on occasion. The most common mistakes are easy to spot when someone else is making them. I call these blunders coaching killers, and here are five to avoid:

- control
- judgment
- projection/ownership
- no value added
- calling other conversations coaching.

Control

Controlling behavior—the need for control, the tendency to control, and the act of controlling the conversation—is the most common and deadliest of the coaching killers. Why do we have to be such control freaks? OK, maybe that is just me, but I imagine that many of you struggle with occasional control issues. If coaching is best pulled by the performer and owned by the performer and measured by the performer, what is there for us to control? Nothing. But I understand that it is often easier to take charge of the conversation, particularly if it seems that the performer is not going to drive progress. It is frustrating to sit back and watch nothing happen.

When we are the coach, we are not the performer. Catalysts help make things easier and do not get consumed in the process. But what if we have been around the block a few times and think we can see what's coming? If invited by the performer, we can share a few stories. But that's all they are: Stories. Examples. Something to think about. If the performer is not interested and engaged, take a step back and ask yourself whether you might be controlling too much of the process and conversation.

Judgment

There are a few different ways to define judgment, and not all judgments are coaching killers. We need good judgment to make decisions and conduct ourselves with maturity and decorum. Here are some aspects of judgment:

- Judgment = an opinion formed by judging something or someone.
- Judgment = assessing a situation or event.
- Judgment = the process of reaching a decision or drawing conclusions.
- Judgment = the ability to draw sound conclusions.

Though it is normal for us to judge people, we need to be wary of judgments that are unhelpful and inaccurate. The worst judgments—the most unhelpful—are often formed based on appearance (such as green-haired and tattooed performers are irresponsible), age (old guys are no longer valuable), style (he's too passive to know what's going on), and background/ethnicity (Americans are self-absorbed, Germans are perfectionists). As a coach, performer, and team member, your goals will be well served if you develop the ability to not judge performers based on these superficial and nontelling characteristics (yes, I know that "nontelling" is not a word, but it should be; appearance, gender, and ethnicity often do not—and should not—indicate stereotypes about a performer's capabilities and tendencies). In chapter 6, I share more about how to learn to embrace diversity and invite people of all ages and backgrounds into your work world.

Projection/Ownership

The projection/ownership coaching killer hits when we take on or take over the ownership of the performer's goals. As a coach we are there to help, but we do not own her performance or goals. Coaches who are results oriented and assertive may have the most trouble staying out of the performer's way. We should own our efficacy as a coach—are we helping the performer, are we being a catalyst, are we letting her pull the coaching process?—but resist becoming a surrogate performer.

Many external coaches base their fees on results—such as, Did the client meet her goals? This is not the same thing as assuming responsibility for the achievement of goals. In fact, projecting a sense of ownership on her goals is a fast way to a lower success rate and payment. Performers will do what they decide to do. Some will make progress, and others will not. As you will read in chapter 4, "The Coachable Coach," I recommend that you help those performers you can and that you don't push too hard on those who do not own their success.

No Value Added

Remember the teacher in the *Peanuts* cartoon shows? She always said, "Wa-waaa-wa-wa-wa-waa." We don't want to be the coach whose words are so inert that they seem like wa-waaa-wa-wa-wa-waa. Time is precious—too precious to waste on a conversation that is not helpful. You might not know the impact that your coaching has right away, but if the performer is not making any progress, you should question whether the coaching is working.

Author's Aside

Peanuts creator Charles Schulz never created adult characters, but the children sometimes respond to the schoolteacher. When they adapted the comic for animation, they continued the focus on the kids by making the teacher's responses inert—the teacher never became a character.

Calling Other Conversations Coaching

The last coaching killer is thinking that you are coaching when you are managing, directing, or counseling. Earlier in the chapter, I distinguished coaching as a helpful conversation driven by the performer. I still hear a lot of managers talk about coaching when they are describing performance counseling—a push conversation that might be helpful but is not necessarily focused on the performer's goals, because the manager wants something specific to change. This is a coaching killer because as long as you think that these managerial conversations constitute coaching, you are less likely to engage in catalytic pull conversations.

Summing Up

These coaching killers can squash a performer's progress and will reduce your impact as a coach. If you find that your conversations with performers are yielding dissatisfactory results—are not helpful—assess your performance and habits against this list of common pitfalls to gain insight about why your well-intended efforts are not working. Great coaching is pulled in by the performer, not pushed onto her by the coach. Though there are many types of helping conversations, learning to discern how coaching can best be catalytic will help you become a more effective coach.

In the next chapter, we're going to shift gears a bit and explore what it means to have four generations in the workplace.

Chapter 2

But I Don't Think Like That

What We Need to Know
About the Generations

I'd like to share a story that has helped many of my training participants get past their natural judgments about the seemingly strange, mean, or frustrating things other people do at work. I was a human resources director at the time, and was working in my office one day when a peer walked in and asked if I had a few moments. I'll call her Sally. Sally closed the door and vented for 10 minutes about how cold and mean our boss—the CEO—was to her. I listened, allowed her to vent, and then asked her for specifics. How did the conversation begin? What was the CEO's response? How did she respond? As Sally recapped the conversation, she shared how the CEO made her feel unvalued and small. Part of the conversation took place over email, and I asked her to show me those emails so that I could get a better feel for what she was describing.

Was Sally's pain real? Yes. Was it appropriate? Who can say. Was it necessary? Not at all. Here is what happened. Sally poured her heart into pitching an idea to the CEO. Her email laid out the reasons why she was proposing an expansion of the programs in her department. Her passion and commitment oozed from her words. She worked hard on her pitch, and she was hoping for a strong and positive response—topped off with a warm "atta-girl." But because she has always felt intimidated by the CEO, she pitched her idea by email—a long email. The CEO sent a three-line response saying he would not consider a program expansion without a full financial analysis of the program's potential revenues and costs. Analysis was not Sally's strong suit, and she took the request for more detail as a personal affront signifying that the CEO did not trust her judgment.

Sally projected her communication style and decision-making preferences onto the CEO and interpreted the CEO's staccato informational response and need for analysis as an indication that he did not care. I see this type of meaning-making all the time, and it is not helpful. Could the CEO have been more sensitive to Sally's need for reinforcement? Sure. But Sally made assumptions about the CEO's response that were neither accurate nor helpful. We all have a filter through which we make sense of the world. Our filter is not the correct one, or only one—it is just ours. To be optimally successful, we need to see other people's filters and communicate with this knowledge in mind.

Sally took a risk by sending her idea by email—a risk that did not pay off. (Sally was not someone who gravitated to technology for most situations, but her fear of the CEO drove her choice of email this day.) Her fear of in-person criticism also led to a disappointment of another kind. Having worked for this CEO for three years, she should have also known that he would need a full analysis (most bosses would want this).

What at first looked like an insensitive response from the CEO was actually an insensitive response from Sally. She was insensitive—and even irresponsible—because she did not communicate in a way that would move her idea forward, and she blamed the CEO for not thinking like her. What do you think? Am I being too hard on Sally?

By the way, the CEO drove me bonkers at times, too. *We all drive each other bonkers.* Our success depends on our ability to separate the daily drama of our clashing communication styles and preferences from the need to effectively convey our ideas to others so they can be understood and used.

Many organizations use assessments to help coworkers get to know each other better—like the Myers-Briggs Type Indicator (which uses psychological dichotomies and types: extraversion/introversion, sensing/intuition, thinking/feeling, and judgment/perception) and DISC (which uses the four dimensions of dominance, influence, steadiness, and conscientiousness). I love these tools because they help us see and distinguish the many ways in which others see the world. And with that knowledge, I hope, also comes the realization that things aren't always as we see them. For example, you might walk into a cocktail party and feel energized and excited. But I would walk into the same gathering and start to plot my exit strategy. We each assign a different meaning and value to the cocktail party—and both our realities are valid.

To give another example: I avoided buying and reading the book *Never Eat Alone* by Keith Ferrazzi (2005) for nearly a year because the title put me off. I love to eat alone, and the thought that I should endeavor to eat with other people to improve my success was not what I wanted to hear. Once I read the book, however, I found that I loved it. Hmmm. . . . This happens with people, too, doesn't it? Once we get to know them, we come to have an entirely different perception.

Our tendency to project our values and definitions onto others also shows up when we work with professionals from different generations. The Baby Boomer says that the green-haired dude wearing jeans while presenting at a meeting is showing disrespect. The green-haired dude interprets the questions coming from the gray-haired dude as a sign of rigidity and that he's stuck in the past. It is likely that the green-haired dude spent hours preparing for the presentation, and this is how he shows respect for the meeting participants' time and attention. And the gray-haired dude who has been there and done that would like to help the new guy not fall flat on his face by making known and tested errors. Instead, two smart and well-meaning people misinterpret and disregard each other.

What if the jeans and green hair were seen as cloth and color and nothing more—meaning nothing in terms of professionalism? What if questions were just questions, and a natural part of any discussion?

The more we can learn about each other, the less likely we will be to assign the wrong meanings and intents to actions and behaviors. And this is why I have set aside this chapter to offer information about each of the four generations in the workplace. I don't want you to memorize the characteristics and generalize about any generation—I want you to see more possibilities for how professionals of all ages approach their work. I want you to think twice before making assumptions that might get in the way of you listening and working well with others.

Our high school and college years are important times in our lives. We start gelling as fully formed—albeit highly flawed (we are still beautifully flawed individuals, but our flaws are more practiced, making us more effectively and rigidly flawed)—human adults, and we launch our independent lives. How we think and define what's normal or strange was shaped by our teen and young adult experiences. Technology played a big role, too, in determining how we did our homework and how we partied. The communication methods and technologies we used when we were young shaped how we thought. They were more than tools—they launched communities.

The medium is the message. In books such as *The Mechanical Bride* (1951/2002) and *The Gutenberg Galaxy* (1962), Marshall McLuhan explored his view that all media are "extensions of man." In fact, that was the subtitle to his most famous book, *Understanding Media* (1964/1994).

In the 1960s and 1970s, rock music became hippies' fuel for activism. Today, social networking media bring the world together in legitimate virtual relationships for today's young professionals.

Given the importance of our teen and young adult years and the dramatic differences for each generation during this time, I thought it would be fun and helpful to explore what high school and college life was like for the Traditionalists, Baby Boomers, Generation Xers, and Millennials. So the rest of this chapter gives snapshots of each generation's experience, with sidebars highlighting a communication icon for teens of the time.

The Traditionalists, Born 1900–1945

> **March 4, 1925: Calvin Coolidge's inauguration is the first to be broadcast nationally over radio.**
>
> *Happy days are here again.*
>
> —Milton Ager and Jack Yellen, 1929

Communications technology in the Traditionalists' formative years:

16-mm film and projector; 78-rpm record; AM radio; blackboard and chalk; carbon paper; cards and letters; cut and paste; drum card; erasable bond paper; handwritten notes; key punch; land-line telephone; long distance; mainframe computer; mimeograph; party line; pen (ball point); pen (ink); pencil; photographic film (black and white); Polaroid camera; record player; rotary dial phone; shorthand; slide rule; Smith-Corona typewriter (manual); telegram

Significant changes in society and culture during the Traditionalists' formative years:

the Depression; jazz, big band, and swing; college rare or interrupted; middle-class growth; military service; a more liberal worldview; the pace of change; World War II; the postwar boom; suburbia; the Bomb

Literacy is widespread among the four age cohorts that I address in this book, but higher education is not. As an example of how raw statistics can be misleading, consider the fact that approximately 28 percent of Americans have a college degree. However, this statistic obscures the fact that higher education is not evenly distributed. Of all the generations, the Traditionalists are the least likely to have a college degree—only 17 percent do.

The Traditionalists absorbed knowledge of their world through the media—traditional newspapers, magazines, and books; and the newer electronic media, which consisted of crude recordings, a growing film industry, and AM radio. Television had been under way in the late 1930s, but World War II delayed its widespread use until the 1950s, so its influence was small during the formative years of even the trailing-edge Traditionalists.

The life experiences of the Traditionalists were shaped by a series of cataclysmic events: World War I; the devastating worldwide outbreak of Spanish influenza beginning in 1918; the stock market crash of 1929, followed by the Great Depression; and World War II. Many Traditionalists mention external events, rather than technology, as key determinants of how their lives would unfold.

The necessity of a broad-based national mobilization to meet these social challenges was mirrored and reinforced by the mass media. People were inundated with messages to enlist, to buy war bonds, to stop the spread of the flu virus, and more. The Traditionalists absorbed these cultural cures

Communication Icon: Typewriters

While my colleagues and I were researching this book, the Traditionalists we contacted mentioned typewriters (sometimes ruefully, sometimes nostalgically) as an example of an important technology during their formative years. Manual typewriters were the order of the day, even though IBM had released an electric model as early as 1934. But that wasn't the main problem; making copies and corrections were. Shorthand rather than electronic recording was used before making a final copy; after that, woe be it to the typist who made mistakes. Erasable bond paper may have been flimsy, but it did allow you to rub out errors, with some difficulty (and then you had to brush away the eraser remnants). Erasure allowed for minor fixes, but major ones required retyping vast sections. Black carbon paper was used to make copies onto a sheet below, as long as the typist struck the keys with even pressure and didn't make too many mistakes. One Traditionalist praised the advent of the copy machine: "It saved me lots of time and trouble—no more need to make carbon copies, especially at the typewriter, where paper tended to slip, with the result that the carbon copies were misaligned. Messy, too. Wasted lots of paper."

and brought them into the workplace: working together for a common good, doing one's duty, thriftiness and responsibility, hard work, loyalty, and respect for rules. Those Traditionalists who are still in the workplace likely hold these values.

The typewriter was an important communication tool for the Traditionalists during their high school and college years. This is somewhat true for Baby Boomers, too, but their typewriters were electric and much easier to use. The Traditionalists plunked down their fingers on the manual keyboard, got blue ink all over themselves messing with real carbon paper, and spent hours making corrections using newfangled erasable bond paper.

●　●　●

I was not a fast and accurate typist. Even with erasable paper, you had to be careful to proofread because it was difficult to get the typewriter back to the exact place to make a correction once the paper was removed. We still have an electric typewriter at my work now for certain tasks and college students often ask what it is and how it works. . . . When I first started using [computers], I had to write my draft out by hand and then put it in the computer, but I still have trouble proofreading on the screen. I have to print copy out consistently to catch typos.

—A Traditionalist

●　●　●

The Baby Boomers, Born 1946–64

January 20, 1961: John F. Kennedy's inauguration is the first to be broadcast nationally over color television

Hope I die before I get old.

—The Who, "My Generation," 1965

Communications technology in the Baby Boomers'
formative years:

33-rpm record; 45-rpm record; 8-track cartridge; analog tape recorder; car stereo; cards and letters; cassette tape; color TV; computer punch card; copy machines; cut and paste; desktop computer; digital clock; DOS; FM stereo; Fortran; handheld calculator; handwritten note; IBM Selectric; interstate highway; land-line telephone; lava lamp; long distance; microwave oven; network television; overhead projector; party line; photographic film (color); record album; reel-to-reel tape recorder; rotary dial phone; rub-off letters; transistor; turntable; typewriter (electric); typewriter (manual); wired remote control; word processing

Significant changes in society and culture during the
Baby Boomers' formative years:

the assassinations of John F. Kennedy, Martin Luther King Jr., and Robert Kennedy; the Beatles and Bob Dylan; the civil rights movement; divorce becomes more common; the military draft and draft lottery; the drug culture; environmental consciousness; folk music; the generation gap; integration; the Kent State shootings; the peace movement; racial and ethnic issues; rock-and-roll; the sexual revolution; the Vietnam War; the volunteer army; the women's movement

The Baby Boomers are certainly the most studied (and self-studied) of the four generations with respect to the workplace. This generation, the largest in American history, grew up with a sense of its own autonomy, which was fed initially by an upbringing rooted in the growing material prosperity of the postwar 1950s, coupled with the ever-present shadow of the Cold War and possible nuclear annihilation. Simultaneously, with the entrance of the Boomers into college in the mid-1960s, a series of extraordinary social changes came about—the civil rights movement, the pill, women's liberation, the assassinations of Kennedy and other leaders, a seemingly interminable and unwinnable war in Vietnam. The impact of all these trends and events was brought into focus by changes in technology and communication that contributed to a generation's sense of itself as unique and different from others, especially from its Traditionalist parents. That sense of independence and self-direction has been seen as the foundation of countercultural alienation in the 1960s, the hedonistic "Me Decade" of the 1970s, and a relentless pursuit of wealth in the 1980s.

Boomers at different ends of the Boomer continuum (the leading versus trailing edge) remember things about their school days a bit differently. As with the Traditionalists, and particularly for older Boomers, the typewriter was still the standard medium of communication, but now it was a bit different.

● ● ●

In high school, our school had no computers. Our keyboarding classes were on typewriters. I remember typing the first papers in high school on a manual typewriter and being thrilled to get an electric typewriter.

—A Boomer

● ● ●

The Boomers were enchanted with the new communication technologies that began flowering during their journey into the ranks of power and influence in society. Most Boomers witnessed a dazzling array of changes from the time of their formal education to their working lives.

● ● ●

During college, I took a computer programming class and used "Punch Cards" to load the program. I had to take the cards to the lab and then wait until the next day to get a report from the computer tech about whether the program had run successfully or not. I remember how exciting it was to be able to program a computer at a terminal and run it immediately.

—A Boomer

● ● ●

Communication Icon: FM Radio

A case could be made for television as the most important driver of technological change for Baby Boomers. McLuhan was certainly thinking of TV when he coined the phrase "global village" to describe the kind of boundary-shrinking that TV screens brought to people's consciousness. Television brought home iconic scenes, such as the first Apollo moon landing in 1969, and disturbing footage of the civil rights movement and the Vietnam War.

Yet in many ways, the older medium of radio was a more powerful determinant of generational identity for Boomers. Music is a powerful creator and reinforcer of group identity. And if there is anything that characterizes Boomers, it is their belief that they are very different from the generations preceding and following them. "Sex, drugs, and rock-and-roll," may not have been part of every Boomer's experience, but nothing conveyed the sense of the Boomers' generation gap from their parents better than the music they chose on the radio. The evolution from the primacy of AM radio in the 1960s to FM in the 1970s mirrors other developments as well. AM radio in its heyday was a true broadcast medium (the term "broadcast" is an agricultural metaphor, referring to seeds widely scattered). Practically every household had one or more radios, and the images of the family gathered around listening to a "fireside chat" by Franklin D. Roosevelt is a powerful icon. But with the growth of FM, radio began to be a narrowcast medium, exploiting relatively small demographic segments with precisely calibrated differences in age, gender, education, and more. The growth of this specialization can be paralleled in the explosion of webpages in the 21st century, each serving its niche.

Early in the Baby Boomers' years of study, such a scheme would normally have been part of the work only of serious mathematics, science, or engineering students. Today, Boomers do this type of analysis on their computers every day. One Boomer remarked that while she had adjusted well to using a computer, "I have repetitive motion injuries from doing it." In fact, worries about health care are increasing concerns as the first wave of Baby Boomers heads toward retirement. Having for the most part prospered during the second half of the 20th century, and expecting that prosperity to continue indefinitely as their nests emptied and their nest eggs swelled, older Boomers are now confronted with worries about the overall economy, inflation, health care, and the continued robustness of their finances. As with the trailing edge of the Traditionalists, many are opting to stay in the workforce longer and find themselves managing, or being managed by, Generation Xers and Millennials.

Generation X, Born 1965–80

> **January 20, 1997: Bill Clinton's second inauguration is the first to be streamed live over the Internet.**
>
> *It's fun to lose and to pretend.*
>
> —Nirvana, "Smells Like Teen Spirit," 1991

Communications technology in Generation X's formative years:

Answering machines; Apple II; Atari; Betamax; cable TV; car phone; CDs; Commodore; computer lab; cordless telephone; desktop; desktop publishing; dial-up; the Internet; laptop computer; laser printer; Macintosh; Microsoft; MTV; online classes; satellite TV; streaming audio; text-only adventure game; VCR; VCR machine rental; VHS; Walkman; whiteboard; Windows; wireless remote control; word processing; World Wide Web; WYSIWYG ("what you see is what you get"; see the glossary at the end of the chapter)

Significant changes in society and culture during Generation X's formative years:

the Gulf War; individualism; job and school combined; parents' divorce; recession; religious awareness; self-discovery; social consciousness; world travel

Because they are media savvy and well educated, the members of Generation X might seem to have advantages that would translate into personal happiness and fulfillment. Yet many of the Gen Xers who shared their experiences with me described a sense of alienation and skepticism. Gen Xers are, after all, a small generation squeezed between much larger ones on either side—a "baby bust." Although they are now entering their peak earning and spending years, many suffer from economic anxiety about their own and their children's futures. Some wonder when the Baby Boomers will begin to step aside for them, and they worry that they will be the first generation in American history to be significantly less well off than the one before.

In terms of technology, the members of Generation X share one overriding commonality: computers. Though many Traditionalists and Baby Boomers have learned to make good use of computers, Generation X is the first to incorporate them fully as a normal part of daily life. Older Gen Xers began using them as part of their formative teen years; many younger ones cannot remember a time when they were not found everywhere.

● ● ●

> At my high school, computers were reserved for students taking special computer and/or math classes. However, because my dad loved computers, we had one in our home from the time I was in 8th grade. The one I remember from high school was a Commodore 64, which my brothers and I used mostly for games. Later I purchased an Atari when going off to college to help with word processing. Both are long gone, but I remember how exciting it was to have them and how wondrous they seemed at the time. Now, I suspect, they would seem impossibly slow and clunky.
>
> —A Gen Xer

● ● ●

Full interactivity for computers would have to wait until the next generation, but the advent of new technologies in the formative years of Generation X was never-ending. This generation saw the first CD players, widespread cable TV, and car phones.

Communication Icon: A Novel and the Computer

The sometimes-frenetic pace of the Generation X lifestyle is reflected in a novel that popularized the name: *Generation X: Tales for an Accelerated Culture,* by the Canadian writer Douglas Coupland (1991). Ironically, the term did not originally refer to the Baby Bust generation but to a segment of the Boomers. Coupland named the book for the band headed by the punk-rock singer Billy Idol. Idol in turn got the name through his mother. In 1964, the writer Jane Deverson had begun a study of English youth for the British magazine *Women's Own,* but her portraits of alienation and behavioral excess were too much for the magazine. Deverson then recruited an American, Charles Hameltt, to help her turn her study into a book, with Hameltt supplying the title Generation X. Idol's mother owned a copy.

Coupland, a late Boomer himself (born in 1961), has resisted being labeled a spokesperson for Generation X. The novel actually began life as a nonfiction study of the post-Boomers, who were then unnamed. Later Coupland explored the new generation's computer users. A study of Microsoft employees he undertook for *Wired* magazine in 1994 resulted in a short article and in another novel, *Microserfs,* for which he immersed himself in the culture of Silicon Valley. The new novel came out the same year that Windows 95 was launched by Microsoft.

Although many Traditionalists and Baby Boomers have learned to make use of computers during their work years, it is Generation X that grew up with the technology. And though he may not be their spokesperson, Coupland's label is the one that has stuck.

Word processing became mainstream. The first computer word processors were really just line editors, designed to allow programmers to make changes in their codes. The first-ever word-processing program in the modern sense was the Electric Pencil, published in 1976 by the programmer Michael Shrayer of Altair. The honor of the first commercially successful such program goes to WordStar, released in 1979 by MicroPro International. It was the best-selling software of the early 1980s. Other early word-processing software were the Apple Write I, Samna III, and Scripsit. The first version of WordStar had been written for the CP/M operating system, which was rapidly replaced by Microsoft's MS/DOS. WordStar for DOS was released in 1982, and by 1985 it was the most popular word-processing software in the world. But within a decade of WordStar's introduction, programs like WordPerfect had knocked it completely out of the market.

The volatility and rapid burnout of WordStar helped set the pattern for the freewheeling days of the early computer wars. Generation X saw the introduction of a bewildering variety of approaches in hardware, software, and peripherals. The first personal computer (PC) as we know it today was the IBM PC in 1981 (which also launched the term "PC"). Atari, Commodore, and even the giant IBM eventually got out of the computer manufacturing business. Microsoft became dominant, thanks to the success of its DOS operating system, plus a lot of marketing savvy and market clout. The pervasiveness of computers, even in such early versions, changed the way Generation X communicated with each other and with the previous generation. Print versus electronic communication set up a technological generation gap that paralleled the values gap of an earlier generation. By the time Generation X was beginning to enter career maturity, newspapers had begun to see their long, slow circulation declines, which have accelerated in the 21st century.

In many ways, the members of Generation X find themselves in the middle. Their values and communication styles set them apart from each.

* * *

My job requires me to continually add to my tech tool kit. For the most part, I am comfortable with this change and really appreciate the way technology has improved my life and my profession. . . . It excites me to think of ways to use technology with teaching while I also deeply love the much older form of technology—the printed book. At times, I feel like I am straddling two worlds.

—A Gen Xer

* * *

The Millennials, Born 1981–99

> **January 20, 2009: Barack Obama's inauguration is the first to be followed nationally on Twitter.**
>
> *Here I am in my little bubble.*
>
> —Coldplay, "Trouble," 2000

Communications technology in the Millennials' formative years:

AOL; broadband; cellphone; dial-up; digital camera; email; Facebook; Google; HD television; instant messenger; iPhone; iPod; LCD projector; LinkedIn; Netbook computer; open source; social networking media; Twitter; video streaming; Web 2.0; web applications; webcam; Wi-Fi; YouTube

Significant changes in society and culture during the Millennials' formative years:

the 9/11 terrorist attacks; the wars in Afghanistan and Iraq; college concerns; economic uncertainty; social connections

As the youngest of the four demographic groups discussed in this book, the Millennials are in some ways still evolving—and their demographic boundaries can be hard to spot. Some demographers date the cohort as beginning in 1977, and others at a later date. And just as with the Baby Boomers, some distinguish differences in the values and attitudes of early and late Millennials.

The Millennials are themselves a kind of boom—a 76-million-strong "Echo Boom" of the original Baby Boomers, who are their parents for the most part. They face intense competition from their peers for colleges, jobs, and houses. But unlike the previous boom, this cohort shows little sign of a generation gap. They share their parents' values and interests to a much greater degree. The most significant differences that set the Millennials apart relate to the incredible explosion of technology

Communication Icon: Social Networking Media

The term "social networking media" has been called "Web 2.0," which sounds like a technological upgrade of the World Wide Web. But Web 2.0 refers to software—a host of new applications that mostly have appeared since the turn of the 21st century. Or perhaps it would be better to say that Web 2.0 is the state of mind that demands, and makes extensive use of, not just passive one-way transfer of information but real interactivity—hosted services, web-based applications, social networking sites, video-serving sites, mash-ups, blogging, and more.

At the time I wrote this book, the three most common sites in use were Facebook, LinkedIn, and Twitter. Facebook has evolved into more of a social friends site, while LinkedIn is favored more for professional contacts. Twitter's instantaneous connections with a network have led to explosive growth, but doubts remain about its role in content. Or perhaps the connections themselves are the content.

By the time you read this, there will very likely be another marvel coming to a piece of electronics very near you—with Millennials showing their online agility. For instance, more and more Millennials—and even the mainstream media—are using word pictures known as tag clouds, which portray the relative frequency of key words in a document. Figure 2-1 gives a tag cloud for this book. And you can make your own tag cloud—visit Tag Crowd (at http://tagcrowd.com).

Figure 2-1. Tag Cloud of This Book

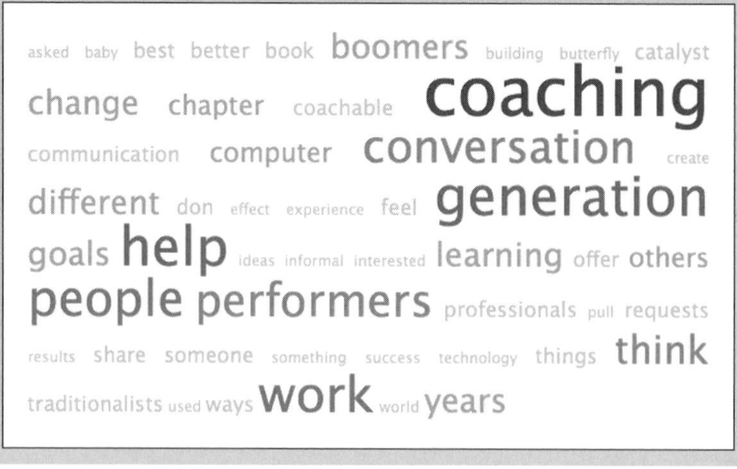

asked baby best better book **boomers** building butterfly catalyst change chapter coachable **coaching** communication computer conversation create different don effect experience feel **generation** goals **help** ideas informal interested learning offer others **people performers** professionals pull requests results share someone something success technology things **think** traditionalists used ways **work** world years that has surrounded them from birth onward. Millennials see things from a global perspective, invoking the connecting power of the World Wide Web. Boundaries between people have become transparent.

The Millennials not only embrace greater tolerance of racial and ethnic diversity; they are also themselves more diverse than their predecessors. By 2010, more than half the U.S. population under 18 will be minorities relative to the population as a whole—and likewise, 1 in 10 will have a parent who is not a U.S. citizen, and 25 percent will be raised by a single parent.

With their souped-up cellphones and blazing Internet connections, the Millennials are the first fully connected generation. Whether sharing music, instant messages, videos, or tweets, the members of this generation are building virtual communities that exceed their physical network. To an even greater degree than the members of Generation X, the Millennials have not simply embraced technology—they have embraced technological change itself.

● ● ●

In both high school and the first two years of college, I relied heavily on dial-up AOL for email and Internet access. Their generated content was typically mediocre, and in those pioneering days of the Internet, general web content wasn't much better. AOL itself has become wholly irrelevant (despite attempts at resurrection), and I now utilize web-based email and direct Internet access through a local broadband ISP.

—A Millennial

● ● ●

Older generations may find themselves smiling ruefully at the thought of the "pioneering" Internet days of just a few years ago. But that is the time viewpoint of the Millennials. And if the web-based application of today doesn't suit, chances are there will be a better one to adopt tomorrow, or perhaps later on this afternoon.

Table 2-1. Examples of How the Cost of Technology Has Changed

Product	Introduced	Initial Cost (dollars)	Cost in 2010 (dollars)	Source Key
Calculator				
K&E 4053-3 slide rule	1910	5	110	1
K&E 68 1617 slide rule	1959	21	154	2
First all-transistor electronic calculator, IBM 608	1957	83,210	646,071	3
First American-made pocket calculator, Bowmar 901B ("Bowmar Brain")	1971	240	1,293	4
Typewriter				
First IBM electric	1934	200	3,256	5
First IBM Selectric	1961	395	2,882	6
Computer				
IBM mainframe 7090	1960	2.9 million	21.4 million	7
IBM 5150 (first personal computer)	1981	1,565	3,756	8
First Apple Macintosh, 128K	1984	1,995	4,189	9
Intel Core Duo system	2010	480	480	10
RAM (per megabyte)				
IBM 5150	1981	39,125	93,908	11
Apple Macintosh, 128K	1984	15,586	32,729	12
Intel Core Duo system	2010	0.24	0.24	13

Sources: The inflation rates are from www.usinflationcalculator.com. The source for each product, by the number in the key above: (1) www.sliderule.ca/4053.htm (based on 1913, not 1910); (2) www.sliderule.ca/4053.htm; (3) www-03.ibm.com/ibm/history/exhibits/vintage/vintage_4506VV2214.html; (4) www.datamath.org/Related/Bowmar/901B.htm; (5) www-03.ibm.com/ibm/history/exhibits/modelb/modelb_prices.html; (6) www-03.ibm.com/ibm/history/exhibits/modelb/modelb_informal.html; and … /exhibits/modelb/modelb_office.html (price unverified); (7) http://en.wikipedia.org/wiki/IBM_7090; (8) www-03.ibm.com/ibm/history/exhibits/pc25/pc25_birth.html; (9) http://en.wikipedia.org/wiki/Macintosh; (10) various online retailers, such as TigerDirect.com; (11) $1,565/.04 (40 kilobytes = .04 megabyte); (12) $1,995/.128 (128 kilobytes = .128 megabyte); (13) $480/2000 (2 gigabytes).

Summing Up

That was a pretty fascinating look backward, wasn't it? Do you get a sense for how our early experiences might shape our assumptions? The title of this chapter is "But I Don't Think Like That" because I think we will be better coaches and performers if we resist attaching judgment and meaning to our different approaches and values. We are all a product of our time—but we also transcend stereotypes and learn new approaches. There is no escaping the fact that our workplaces are full of hard-working, dedicated professionals whose lives were formed by radically different experiences.

This blending of realities is very cool, in fact. In this same vein, here are two more collections of information, just for the fun of it. First, take a look at the glossary of terms in the sidebar below. Which words do you know and identify with? I'll bet you instantly recognized the terms that define your generation. And check out table 2-1, to see how the cost of technology has changed.

So far, we've explored the fundamentals of coaching and the young adult experiences of four generations. In the next chapter, we will consider these two topics together to discover how we can better coach and be coached, up and down the generations.

Glossary of Terms—Most Mentioned in This Chapter

aggregator. An RSS feed (see below) reader that automatically checks your subscribed feeds regularly for content and downloads them to your computer or mobile device.

analog. Any recording method whereby a signal of some kind is recorded in direct proportion to the volume, pitch, and other characteristics of the original audio source. Typically refers to recordings made onto vinyl such as LPs, film, or audiotape.

Atari. An early, and at one time leading, manufacturer of video games and consoles as well as computers (first produced in 1979).

Beta(max). Video recording technology developed by Sony. Eventually supplanted in consumer use by the similar but physically incompatible VHS technology.

carbon paper. Paper with black ink on one side. When placed between two pieces of white paper, a somewhat fuzzy "carbon copy" would be made on the lower page when the upper was struck by typewriter keys.

card catalog. A set of cards in small drawers describing the contents of a library and the location of the materials in question in the stacks. Typically in three parts—author, title, and subject matter. Since replaced by computer databases.

cassette. Recording method using magnetic tape wound onto two reels and enclosed in a cartridge. Could refer to audio or video recordings. Unlike 8-tracks, the tape could be rewound or fast-forwarded. Audio recordings could be flipped over at the end to provide twice the length.

Commodore. Early series of home computers. Models were the PET (1977), VIC-20, and 64.

cut and paste. Term from mechanical layouts in the printing industry. Bits of printed text would literally be cut with scissors, positioned by hand and fixed with glue. The concepts and terms continued in the computer era in the first word processors.

dial-up. Method of connecting a home computer to the Internet via a telephone line. Line tie-ups, slow speeds, and the consequent lack of ability to transmit large files have caused this technology to be supplanted by the faster, always-on technology called broadband.

digital. Method of recording and storing data as strings of binary numbers (0s and 1s) rather than analog wave forms. The strings can be stored electronically or on a physical medium such as tape.

DOS. Disk operating system: The set of digital instructions that tells a computer how to operate. There have been many flavors of DOS, by far the best known being Microsoft's MS-DOS.

DVR. Digital video recorder: A device that stores digital images or programs, typically from cable or satellite systems, on a computer disk for later playback.

8-track. Tape playback mechanism that uses songs prerecorded onto cartridges wound with a continuous loop of tape. Each loop has four separate sections of two tracks each for stereo. The predecessor of the cassette tape.

erasable bond paper. Type of paper used before the invention of copiers. It was a sheet of thin paper that was (relatively) easy to erase when a typing error had been made.

film. Medium for storing analog still pictures.

Fortran. Early example of a computer programming language.

GPS. Global Positioning System: A space-based radio-navigation system for determining location, including both geographical coordinates and elevation, that uses triangulated satellite signals and is operated by the U.S. government. "GPS" is also used for the unit providing such information.

HTML code. Hypertext Markup Language: The predominant markup language for webpages and blog posts.

IM. Instant messaging—better known as IM or IMing, in Internet slang—allows you to send real-time messages to individuals on your buddy or contact list. You type messages to each other into a small window that shows up on your screen and your buddy's screen. It is like a typed telephone call.

iPod. The most widely used storage/playback device for mp3 files, and later, for video and still pictures. A trademarked term for an Apple product, but which has given its name to podcasting and other forms of communication.

land line. Telephone service in homes and other buildings based on wiring coming in to the structure, with fixed locations for telephone units. A complement to the portability of cellphones, and in many instances being replaced by them.

LP. Short for long-playing record album, the standard medium for longer or multisong recordings, played at 33 rpm. Each side could hold about 25 minutes of audio. LP art became an important part of the image of bands and recordings during their heyday, from the late 1940s until the advent of CDs. Some artists still release LPs.

mimeograph. Short for mimeograph machine, a type of simple printing press that forces ink through a master sheet produced on a typewriter. Supplanted by the advent of low-cost copying and offset printing, but still used in some developing countries because it does not require electricity to run.

mp3. A compression algorithm for producing much smaller audio files than ones that capture the maximum information produced by digital sampling.

MS-DOS. See DOS.

party line. An older type of telephone exchange with several different numbers sharing one connection. When one party was on the line, others had to wait their turn (and occasionally eavesdrop).

podcast. Audio segments delivered via RSS feed (see below) to iPods and other portable media players.

punch card. A medium for data entry made up of stiff paper with spaces missing or present in predetermined locations. Used in early computer data input. In the 19th century, the ancestors of computer punch cards were used to drive industrial machinery, such as looms. Descendants are sometimes used in voting machines.

reel-to-reel. Transport mechanism for storing magnetic tape used for recording and playback of video, audio, and data. Small versions were used in cassettes, larger ones were used in professional machines, and very large ones were used in mainframe computers. Differs from 8-track in that the tape can move backward and forward.

rotary dial. Signaling input device for older analog phones. A dial is turned a specified distance and released to return; the number of clicks heard lets the system know which numeral is meant.

RSS. Really Simple Syndication: A format for notifying users when content has been updated on your subscribed list of websites, blogs, and podcasts. An RSS feed is how you receive an RSS document, which is called a "feed" or "channel," and contains either a summary of content from an associated website or the full text.

search engine optimization. The process of increasing desirable traffic to a website.

second life. A virtual world. I know several professionals who have set up virtual meeting rooms in their virtual worlds. Their avatars meet about real business problems and then tell their human equivalents what was decided; see http://secondlife.com.

Selectric. Electric typewriter model first introduced by IBM in 1961. Among its innovations were a type roller that stayed horizontally stationary while the typehead moved, in contrast to almost all other manual and electric designs, and a "typeball" that rotated to strike the paper and could be interchanged for different typefaces. The Selectric eventually accounted for 75 percent of all typewriter use in the U.S. business market.

78. The number of revolutions per minute (rpm) of record albums and singles before 45s and LPs. Used for both pop and classical music, the latter requiring multiple separate discs, because a side could only play for about four minutes.

shorthand. A method of taking verbatim dictation manually by means of symbols; a valuable skill in the days before widespread voice recording.

Skype. This very popular VoIP (see below) provider lets you make free calls over the Internet to anyone else who also has the service.

slide rule. A device used primarily by scientists and engineers to calculate multiples of large numbers; in effect, a small mechanical analog computer. It contained three segments, usually of wood, with the middle segment capable of sliding side to side, and numbers arranged logarithmically. It made use of the fact that adding exponents of numbers (by lining one up over another) is the same as multiplying them. Essentially supplanted by electronic calculators in the 1970s.

social networking. The term used to describe participation in online communities and online relationship building.

stacks. In libraries, the physical shelves that store books and other sources. Stacks are numbered according to the catalog system employed by the library housing them.

33—more precisely, 33-1/3. The number of revolutions per minute (rpm) of long-playing 12-inch record albums (LPs).

turntable. The surface on which an LP, 45, or 78 record turns while a stylus tracks the grooves in the record. A record player uses a turntable and contains electronics and speakers for amplification.

Twitter. A combination of blogs, IM, and the cellphone. People post about what they are doing—mowing the grass, reading blogs, painting toenails.

typewriter. A device that writes on paper. When a user strikes a key, it activates (either mechanically or electrically) a mechanism that presses an ink ribbon against the paper, leaving a specific image on the page. See Selectric.

VCR. Videocassette recorder: A device for recording and playing back video, storing the data on magnetic tape. Familiar types include VHS and (earlier) Betamax.

VHS. The principal type of VCR during its heyday. A VHS cassette normally held between 2 and 6 hours of video, depending on the tape speed chosen.

viral. Refers to viral marketing or to similar techniques that increase product or brand awareness through word-of-mouth communication or their online equivalents.

VoIP. Voice-over-Internet Protocol, which is used for Internet telephony (like Skype and Vonage).

Walkman. A popular audio device introduced by Sony in 1979 that first made music truly portable for the user. It originally designated a cassette player (sometimes with an FM radio) and was later extended to other digital media, both audio and video.

Weblog/blog. Websites that utilize specialized software to make adding and updating content quick and easy (many blogs are updated on a daily basis). They are often described as online journals featuring news articles and links to other blogs.

wiki. An open, collaborative website where users and/or contributors can add, remove, and edit content using a web browser.

wired remote. A device for operating a television at a distance to change channels, adjust volume, and so on. Since supplanted by wireless versions.

WordStar. The first commercially successful word processor software, introduced in 1979.

WYSIWYG. An acronym for "What you see is what you get": Said of the first page-layout and word-processing software that attempted to display on screen the actual look of a printed page. Usually referred to text editors that showed the formatting of text and enabled people to post good-looking content on the web without knowing HTML code (see above).

You Tube. A popular website where anyone can upload and watch videos.

Chapter 3

Up, Down, and Sideways

Coaching That Transcends Generational Differences

In researching this book, I conducted a survey of about 200 professionals from the four generations—Traditionalists, Baby Boomers, Generation X, and Millennials—about their coaching preferences. I was curious to see the differences I would find, and I was excited at the prospect of sharing these findings with you. Well, I won't be sharing much from this survey, because I found very little worth telling, except that people of all ages seem to have practically identical coaching preferences—there were no notable differences! I can't say that I am surprised, because we all want to own our learning.

I have talked with hundreds of people about coaching, and when I combine their feedback with the information from the survey I conducted, several important themes emerge. First, performers want to be respected and want to be coached by people who are pleasant and likable. How we come across is critical. Performers don't want to feel manipulated or that you have an ulterior motive or some predefined purpose. They don't want you to take over the conversation. Performers from all four generations emphasized that they don't want to be approached by would-be coaches when they are busy (emphasizing the benefits of a pull coaching approach). And many performers said they preferred a direct approach when receiving feedback.

Because there seem to be no differences in coaching preferences across the generations, this chapter is not needed, right? I wish that were true. Just because we all want the same open and flexible treatment from coaches does not mean that we are all adequately connecting up and down the generations. This is a big challenge, and so it is the focus of this chapter. How can we build better relationships with people who are older or younger than us so that we can help each other grow and succeed? To begin answering this question, the two sections of this chapter offer coaching suggestions. The first section offers a profile of the agile coach and suggests how coaches can become more catalytic in a workplace filled with professionals from the four generations. The second section revisits the culture and context from which each generation has come and considers how their varying histories might affect performers' responses to coaching.

The Agile Coach

If you have read the previous chapters, you will have come to the conclusion that above all else, I am suggesting that coaches need to be as nimble as Gumby. The enigmatic nature of people and breakthrough science limit how much a defined and rigid approach can work. Coaching is a complex skill that requires us to constantly make and remake judgments about how we can best help each performer. Here are four practices of the agile coach:

- Be the one to bend.
- Believe in others.
- Be real.
- Take the initiative to seek coaching from diverse performers.

Being the One to Bend

Perhaps you have observed situations in which two professionals fail to connect because neither will take the first step to understand the other.

They let their egos, pride, or sense of what's right get in the way of taking the first step to build a relationship, and they let first impressions or stereotypes define their opinions about their colleagues. To avoid this type of impasse, when building or rebuilding a relationship, someone must go first, and I am suggesting that you be that one.

You need to be the one to show your interest in the performer. You need to be the one to ask about her communication preferences and goals. And you need to be the one to demonstrate what openness looks like in practice. Green hair? No problem. You'd like to meet over Skype? That's fine, if you show me how (show her that you are really interested in learning). You'd enjoy swapping blog posts and discussing the latest TED video over yerba mate? Sounds interesting; count me in!

The strategy of being willing to be the one to bend also applies to conflict situations. As a coach, you cannot influence people with whom you have a strained relationship. Be the one to check in on her and extend an olive branch—even if you think you are right and she is wrong. Show that you are interested in doing whatever it takes to build a good working relationship. If you take the first step, she will follow and meet you halfway.

Believing in Others

In chapter 1, I suggested that coaches assume the "sponge stance"—a listening method based on feeling admiration and interest for another. The story I shared asked you to assume that the person in line at Starbucks was someone you admired. Here I want to take this idea one step further and ask you to see all performers as amazing and worth your admiration. How would your coaching be different if everyone you coached was a committed, engaged, passionate, and talented professional? Well, guess what: They are! If you believe in the capacity of people to grow, change, and excel, you will come across in a more helpful way. The agile coach sees excellence in everyone. See the sidebar for a blog post I wrote a few years ago on this topic.

You Are Amazing, Even If Today You Are Off Course

You are amazing. I know this! If you and I enjoyed a chat over foaming lattes, I am sure that your greatness would shine bright, and I would find your hopes and dreams inspiring. Everyone I meet possesses clear and special talents. I love to discover the source of people's passions and am fascinated by our diverse natures.

Every night on TV, we see people are at their best, but more often they are at their worst (crime shows, reality TV, Jerry Springer). If everyone is amazing, what's going on? I think that stress and the dizzying circumstances of our lives can push us off course. We know this is not how things ought to be. We know that we have something greater and more compelling to offer the world. Even so, we get farther off course with each mismatched turn.

You are amazing, even if today you are off course.

You have the potential to contribute to society and live a wonderful and fulfilling life. You can get back on track. I work with many people who choose to stop moving in the wrong direction and see a new set of possibilities. They flap their butterfly wings fast and furious, manifesting joy and wonder along the way. They ooze exuberance and become flexibly strong, like a tall Sequoia tree swaying in the wind. They become like an awesome force of nature. What's your goal? Do you need an adjustment?

- You can start right now: Define. Answer. Act. Use that energy to repeat.
- What can I do in the next 12 hours to get unstuck? (Do one big or five tiny things, then rejoice.)
- Which is more powerful—physical or mental barriers? (Hint: It's likely mental; obliterate the barriers by taking on a new perspective.)
- What two things can I do for the next five days to get back on track?

We all get off course sometimes, and that does not make us any less amazing—we're like Ferrari sports cars parked in our garages, not performing because the engine is off. Turn the key and go for a ride.

Source: http://managementcraft.typepad.com/2weeks2abreakthrough/
2007/01/you_are_amazing.html.

When we believe in and admire performers, we interact with them in noticeably different ways. Think about the people with whom you work—it is likely quite obvious to you which individuals admire and value you and believe in your ability to produce success. And I would bet that you respond very differently to your admiring fans than you do to people who seem less interested in what you are doing. Be that admiring fan for others, and expand your opportunities to make a positive difference for them.

Being Real

The American psychologist Carl Rogers was one of the founders of humanistic psychology and perhaps best known for his work on person-centered therapy, which found wide application in various environments, including the workplace. Rogers was given the Award for Distinguished Professional Contributions to Psychology by the American Psychological Association in 1972, and he was nominated for the Nobel Peace Prize for his work with national intergroup conflict in South Africa and Northern Ireland. He wrote extensively about the dynamics of the helping field, and I think that coaches—although not working in a clinical setting—can learn a lot from his research. Here is a quotation from his best-selling book *On Becoming a Person* about the importance of trust in a helping relationship:

> Can I be in some way which will be perceived by the other person as trustworthy, as dependable or consistent in some deep sense? Both research and experience indicate that this is very important, and over the years I have found what I believe are deeper and better ways of answering this question. I used to feel that if I fulfilled all the outer conditions of trustworthiness—keeping appointments, respecting the confidential nature of the interviews, etc.—and if I acted consistently the same during the interviews, then this condition would be fulfilled. But experience drove home the fact that to act consistently acceptant, for example, if in fact I was feeling annoyed or skeptical or some other non-acceptant feeling, was certain in the long run to be perceived

as inconsistent or untrustworthy. I have come to recognize that being trustworthy does not demand that I be rigidly consistent but that I be dependably real. (Rogers 1995, 119)

Wow—this is very useful. Dependably real. . . . Hmmm . . . What does that look like at 10 in the morning? In a staff meeting? When you think someone screwed up? When you're coaching a performer who is playing the victim? When your boss is being superficially "consistent"? When you have failed or messed up?

The hard part, of course, is learning how to be dependably real in ways that you don't regret later (or that put others off or cause them to become uncoachable). And for those of you who are recovering control freaks like me, we need to learn how we can be real while resisting the urge to over-assert our notions (and thereby become dependably obnoxious).

Authenticity is so valuable. Being humble and interested in others is important for building trust. Self-absorption or aggression dressed in a costume called "being real" is not. Our challenge and opportunity: How can we be focused on helping others while also showing our emotions and vulnerabilities (and thus using emotional intelligence)?

One more thing from the legendary Carl Rogers: His research of effective person-centered therapy indicated that the best therapists were not necessarily the most schooled or classically trained. The best therapists had two things in common: They did not overcontrol the helping relationship, and they were more authentic and sensitive. This holds true in the world of business, too. The best coaches are agile and open relationship builders, first and foremost. When we bring together a service orientation and authenticity, we become more effective coaches.

Taking the Initiative to Seek Coaching from Diverse Performers

The final suggestion brings together a lot of what I have written about in previous sections of the book. The more you practice communicating, connecting, and collaborating with performers of all ages, the better you will understand your challenges and opportunities. The more you seek and receive coaching from colleagues unlike you, the better you will be able to influence other performers. The more you learn about diverse styles and preferences, the better you will be able to adjust your style and be heard as you intend.

There is no better way to learn than to seek coaching, and I invite you to go first—be the one to initiate a more lively and interesting mix of conversations. Each coaching conversation you pull will have the potential to become an opportunity for you to reciprocate and provide coaching. Coaching up and down the generations starts with coachable and curious performers.

The agile coach is happy to be the one to bend, because she believes that people are worthy of her admiration, she is dependably real, and she herself takes the initiative to seek coaching from a broad variety of professionals. Her resolve is strong, and her rigidity is low. She knows that there are many ways to build relationships, and she stays focused on the quality of the connection.

The Generations—Take Two

Let's add another layer of information for how you can best coach up and down the generations. Being agile is critical, and you may need to flex your style or approach in recognition of the times from which the performer comes. Here is more contextual information that you can consider when coaching performers from the four different generations.

The Traditionalists

Even those Traditionalists who have retired or are about to do so have not necessarily ended their working careers. Relatively good health, longer life spans, and economic uncertainties will likely cause many to begin a new job, or to volunteer in a significant way for causes they believe in. Far from being averse to technology, many Traditionalists have eagerly embraced the Internet as a way to keep in touch with grandchildren, classmates, former service buddies, and the like. Still, those from younger generations who work with or who find themselves coaching Traditionalists in such roles need to understand the best modes of communication with this group. For example, many Gen Xers and Millennials are much more used to multitasking and to interactive, near-constant feedback. To a Traditionalist with a "no news is good news" mentality, such feedback can seem like nothing more than an interruption. It's not that there is no room for feedback, but Traditionalists may feel strongly that there is a proper time and place for it. What a Gen Xer might see as immediate and honest can seem hasty and inappropriate to an older worker.

To turn matters around, younger workers being coached or supervised by Traditionalists may react negatively to feedback that seems excessively formal, heavy-handed, or "preachy." But to the Traditionalists, such an approach may seem perfectly appropriate and in line with the rules of the workplace as they have lived them. As a younger performer, don't get put off by this higher level of preparation and formality—be thankful for the coaching and for the time and energy the coach gave on your behalf.

The Baby Boomers

A great deal has been written about the nature and values of the Baby Boomers—much of it contradictory. Take idealism, for example. Whether or not Boomers are indeed more idealistic than other generations may be debated, but it's probably safe to say that Boomers see themselves as more idealistic. The countercultural angst of the 1960s was not so much a rejection of traditional American values as it was a critique of the previous generation for not living up to those values. As Boomers age and mature, they have shown themselves willing to move into societal roles that they once might have scorned.

This entire progression was brilliantly captured by the humorist Dave Barry (1990, 119): "You don't need a weatherman to know that harsh sunlight can harm your BMW's finish." Readers who understand Barry's 1960s reference can skip this paragraph, but for others: Barry is deliberately inverting the signature line from Bob Dylan's 1965 song "Subterranean Homesick Blues": "You don't need a weatherman to know which way the wind blows." It's classic Dylan—mysterious, paranoid, lyrical, and prosaic all at once. The radical 1960s protest group the Weathermen (later the Weather Underground) took its name from Dylan's line. And today some of them are indeed probably driving BMWs.

In working with Baby Boomers, then, a key touchstone is often that sense of idealism and optimism. Having seen the American Dream from below and above, Boomers remain optimistic about it, for both themselves and their descendants. The pervasive technologies that were so much a part of their formative years—like television, radio, and record albums—all contributed to their sense of identity with their age cohort and their desire to belong to a larger cause. Having fought hard to get into college, they're competitive, yes, but competitive in wanting to put their stamp on things. And they don't want simply to do a job; they also want the personal gratification and fulfillment that come from making a difference.

As coaches for Generation X performers, Baby Boomers may find themselves at odds with what appear to be skeptical or disillusioned responses and attitudes. Compared with Boomers, Generation X is much smaller, and opportunities for career advancement may seem to be thwarted by a generation unwilling to relinquish either power or what may seem their sense of entitlement to a special place in the scheme of things.

Baby Boomers tend to give themselves over to their jobs. They believe in paying dues, playing by the rules, and building careers. Their feedback and guidance are indirect and are considerate of people's feelings. They're process oriented. They are trained to believe that business results and relationships are intertwined. To get ahead, Boomers learned to be diplomatic and to believe in people skills. Their sense of who they are is deeply connected to their career achievements. They have a sense of entitlement, are optimistic, are cynical toward institutions, and believe in endless youth.

Generation X

In the contemporary workplace, the Traditionalists and Baby Boomers more often think of themselves as coaches of Generation Xers rather than the other way around. But, as I suggested earlier in the book, I think that all generations can and should learn from each other. That said, it would not be uncommon to find older workers assuming that they ought to offer coaching to younger workers. This could put off younger workers, who do not want to be talked down to or made to feel less valuable in the workplace. In such a setting, the potential is high for differing values and styles of communication to clash. To avoid this conflict, each generation, especially when the coach is older and is the manager, must recognize the different styles used by the other.

Generation Xers value teamwork and seek a fun and informal workplace. They expect employees at all levels and ages to be valued equally. They don't want to be micromanaged, and they have a strong preference for pull coaching. When coaching a Gen X performer, give her bursts of help and then let her go off and work on it. She will likely come back to you quickly with an update and will appreciate your positive reinforcement. Gen Xers value a work/life balance and coaching that can help them become a well-rounded success.

The Millennials

As the Millennials move steadily into the workforce, accompanied by the retirements of Traditionalists and Baby Boomers, it is important for coaches to know how many performers of this generation process information and how they prefer to work. Because they tend to be well educated and technologically advanced, the Millennials are less likely to be loyal to any one company or industry. They are adept at building global virtual relationships, and many have an independent contractor mentality (or that of a guru, free agent, or solopreneur). Millennial performers will likely value philanthropy and volunteerism—doing good for others—although this may not translate into a broader goodwill for the corporation. They are natural-born multitaskers who may intimidate or irritate older coaches and performers with their "always connected" way of life. If you want to connect to a Millennial, do so using their preferred technology tools (versus the weekly one-to-one).

Coaches who work with Millennials should keep in mind that their goals are probably not bound by real or virtual borders—they can work anywhere and reinvent their approach very quickly. Coaches that seem change resistant will find it tough to connect with this generation. This generation is used to giving and getting feedback in real time, and thus they may expect constant feedback from managers and coaches, which older professionals may find uncomfortable or undesirable. And older performers being coached by Millennials might desire a more methodical approach.

Summing Up

As a coach, you should seek to understand and empathize with the points of view of all performers. You will be more effective if you approach coaching as an opportunity to connect with coworkers from all walks of life, and you will be able to create a more positive and coachable environment by leading the way and actively seeking coaching from professionals who are both older and younger than you.

In the next chapter, we'll examine how leaders and development professionals can affect whether and how well coaching up and down the generations can be done.

Chapter 4

The Coachable Coach

When I think about the people I most admire, I realize that many of them model coachability in ways that make them seem wise. That's an interesting concept, isn't it? That being coachable (a learner) might make us seem wise (someone who knows). It is not the acquisition of knowledge, facts, or experience that distinguishes us but our unending quest for learning and our openness to improving.

If you want to be the best possible coach, you need to be highly coachable. Many moons ago, I set out to do a master's thesis on coachability. My premise was that coachability was a larger lever to pull than coaching skills. In other words, if you could only do one thing—help people be better coaches or help people be more coachable—an organization would get a better return on effort and resources by providing training on and reinforcing coachability. As it is with most thesis papers, I needed to find and cite many references that either supported or refuted my hypothesis. I ended up abandoning the idea. Why? Not because my hypothesis proved false—on the contrary, I believe it more today than ever. I had to abandon the idea for the thesis because I could not find any—not one—resources that addressed coachability. This was extraordinary! I could find thousands of books with tips on how to be a great coach and not one that told me how to be coachable.

I started writing about coachability more than 10 years ago, and I try to address some aspect of it in every book. I believe it is that powerful! Practicing coachability has changed my life and opened up many opportunities. If you want to be a great coach (manager, parent, friend, innovator, and the like), you need to be highly coachable. Being coachable will improve every aspect of your work and life.

Coachability

What do I mean by coachability? Coachability is the degree that we are open to what the environment can offer or the extent to which we accept and consider input and ideas. Our successes depend on whether we are highly coachable when it counts most. Coachability is a way of behaving, not a characteristic—there are no coachable or uncoachable people, just moments when a person is either coachable or uncoachable. Although everyone is coachable some of the time and uncoachable at other times, the most effective professionals will be more coachable overall and, most important, at the times when they need to learn from others. Table 4-1 describes signs that suggest whether someone is being coachable or uncoachable.

I also want to address what coachability and uncoachability feel like, because this is a powerful distinction. Imagine that you are being uncoachable. You have put up an imaginary barrier between you and the person who is trying to help you. You feel this invisible wall; it is crushing your spirit. It feels stressful; your brow wrinkles and your stomach tightens. You are sending bad chemicals surging through your veins as the stress response kicks into high gear. Being uncoachable does not feel good.

Being coachable, on the other hand, can feel great. You feel a sense of confidence, even when the topic of discussion is critical. You are relaxed and feel a professional affection for the other person; after all, she is giving you the gift of her time and feedback. And when the feedback is really helpful, you feel a rush of excitement and enthusiasm. Aha and eureka moments come when you are coachable. Coachability feels great.

Table 4-1. What Coachability Looks Like

Coachable	Uncoachable
Is not defensive when offered an alternative point of view	Staunchly defends current decisions, practices, and ideas
Welcomes ideas and feedback about ways to improve	Does not listen to suggestions offered by others
Asks for coaching	Appears nonreceptive or not interested in coaching
Reflects on and uses ideas that others offer	Does not use the ideas that others offer; may be dismissive of others
Looks for development opportunities, whether in the form of reading, classes, new assignments, or coaching from others	Does not seek self-development nor engage in conversations about self-development
Is open to acknowledging strengths and weaknesses	Believes that asking for input is a sign of weakness; is uncomfortable acknowledging and discussing weaknesses
Handles failures and setbacks with grace and honesty	Is defensive and looks for someone to blame; may hide mistakes rather than openly discuss them
Has confidence and an ownership for results	Is driven to be right

Start to tune your senses for coachability. Begin noticing what coachability and uncoachability look like in other people and in your own behavior. Observe how you react to others and how they react to you. What barriers are you erecting, and how does it feel when you are being uncoachable? Why have you placed the barrier there? Notice how personality, time of day, and topic affect your coachability. In meetings, observe what the meeting leader does that helps or hinders the coachability of the attendees.

When we are coachable, there is an open, curious, and relaxed quality to our demeanor. Being coachable goes hand in hand with confidence and an ownership of results. Coachable coaches display a sense of calm and a focus that allows them to better help performers without feeling the need to defend or rationalize their ideas or past actions.

The bad news is that many people spend more time being uncoachable than coachable. The good news is that coachability is a state of mind that can be changed in an instant—yes, an instant. Like this—pow! How? Pardon my bluntness, but we need to get over ourselves, drop the judgment, and hold ourselves to a higher standard as a performer. See and feel the wall you are putting up between you and others, call it a wall, and then blast the wall away by choosing to hear the help being offered as a wonderful gift. It might be a painful gift, but any time someone takes the time and energy to help you, it is something to be open to and thankful for. And don't worry about the perfection—or imperfection— of their delivery. People have told me that they don't like advice that sounds a particular way. Remember, we all have different filters, and so our ways of trying to help will differ. Don't let the tone of someone's voice get in the way. We can and should learn to spot situations that, and people who, trigger our uncoachability or conversely improve our responses and enhance learning.

Learning is like breathing. When we stop, we can no longer be effective, and we become irrelevant in the workplace. Think back to chapter 1: Wa-waa-wa-wa-wa-waa. Now consider the sidebar.

Coaching the Uncoachable

It is a waste of time to try to coach performers who are being uncoachable, which is another reason to let performers own their learning. If you know someone who is often uncoachable, share this chapter with her, and hopefully a proverbial lightbulb or two will come on for her. The information will be best received if you share a story about your goals to become a more coachable person. Be humble, and the world will see you as wise.

If a performer is being uncoachable, your goal should be to help her become coachable. Here are several techniques to encourage and improve coachability:

Lisa's Proverbial Two-by-Four Whack Over Her Head

Have you ever been given such hard-to-hear feedback that it felt as if you had been hit between the eyes with a two-by-four board? I have, and it saved my career. It happened more than 10 years ago. My boss told me that I was egotistical, a know-it-all, defensive, and uncoachable—and that several people had told her they did not like to work with me. Wow. Shock. And as you would expect from a young egotistical know-it-all, I concluded that I had a bad boss. I was defensive and demonstrated every behavior of which she was accusing me (I did not see this at the time). Over the next several days, her words sank in and became weighty.

My boss was right. Once I saw how uncoachable I was being, I was able to change in an instant. I redefined my success as being someone others regarded as open, coachable, and a pleasure to work with. My demeanor changed immediately, and new possibilities emerged. Today's reality would look much different had I not received that benevolent whack between the eyes. What a gift!

What my boss gave me was not coaching; it was performance counseling. I share this story here to illustrate the powerful nature of coachability and to invite you to pay attention to any proverbial two-by-fours that might come your way at some point in your career. If someone takes the time and demonstrates the courage to offer direct feedback, be sure to show your gratitude. It might not be easy to hear, but the proverbial two-by-four can jolt you onto the right track if you are coachable. Offered with good intent and care, the proverbial two-by-four can catalyze a breakthrough. And sometimes a breakthrough begins with alienation.

- Communicate in ways and using vehicles that appeal to performers. Do they prefer direct one-to-one communication, or are they more receptive to hearing stories and examples? What role does technology play in their daily work life?
- Use learning techniques and methods that best suit their style and behavioral tendencies.
- Talk about coachability as a catalyst for success. Performers who understand coachability will be more open to coaching.

- When you notice that a performer is being uncoachable, ask if she would prefer to reschedule the conversation. Explain that she seems distracted or deep in thought and that you'd be happy to come back another time.
- Talk openly about coachability triggers and share yours. Suggest that performers notice when they feel a wall of resistance, and then pause, take a deep breath, and decide to let go of the feelings and be more open.
- Ask open-ended questions that get performers talking about their goals. Talk about things that are important to them.
- Be open about the triggers you see. Share the techniques that you use to be more coachable.

Summing Up

Cultivating and developing coachability is a craft, and we can get better at it over time if we try. I believe that being coachable is a significant lever for success and one of the most meaningful developmental journeys we can take as a coach and performer.

In the next chapter, we'll explore several ways to catalyze breakthroughs and help performers zoom forward in ways they may not imagine are possible.

Chapter 5

Extra Credit

The Science
of Breakthroughs

I've called this chapter "Extra Credit" because it offers ways to improve your impact as a coach after you are consistently practicing the fundamentals outlined in chapters 1 and 3. I became interested in the nature of generating breakthroughs in performance about 10 years ago and have experimented with and written about many techniques for creating a step change in progress. That's how I define the breakthrough experience—as scooting up a step forward that is higher and longer than what would happen with continuous improvement, as pictured in figure 5-1.

The term "breakthrough" means different things to different people. Some reserve the word for describing scientific discoveries and efforts worthy of the Nobel Prize. Others believe they have breakthrough experiences many times a week; they might look like this:

- A moment when the performer has an insight, aha moment, brilliant idea, cognitive snap (relative to the preceding time period), or epiphany.
- Exciting progress experienced by an individual or small group.

- A discontinuous positive change, or a leap forward in thinking, action, or results.
- A change that can be small or large, but there must be an acceleration of progress or sudden insight (transformative versus incremental).

When it comes to breakthroughs, it is all about momentum; and to generate momentum, it is helpful to believe in the big power of small actions. The next section, which is adapted from an essay I wrote about the "butterfly effect," can serve as a good foundation for understanding the breakthrough techniques that are explained later in this chapter. (This essay was originally published on my blog, Management Craft, at www.managementcraft.com, on April 15, 2008.)

The Butterfly Effect

In a world that is focused on big things—big business mergers, box office hits, platinum music CDs, supermodels, best-selling books, Humvees, big

Figure 5-1. The Breakthrough Experience (BKE) Compared with Continuous Improvement

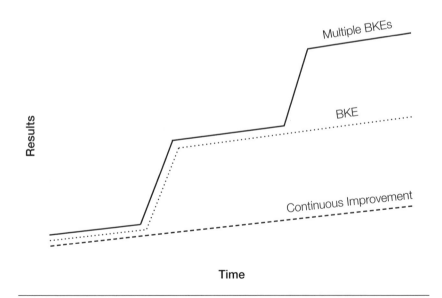

box retailers—it's nice to contemplate the power of the very small. Even more satisfying is the notion that small might be greater than big.

The butterfly effect is a popularized interpretation of one of the key elements of chaos theory and has its roots in something that mathematicians refer to as extreme sensitivity to initial conditions: the fact that small and seemingly insignificant changes at the start of a process can produce wildly different and practically unpredictable results—see the sidebar for the details.

Simply put, the butterfly effect is the notion that something as small as a flap of a butterfly's wings can make a big impact—like causing a tornado on the other side of the world. The flapping wings move the air, and the effect reverberates. If the butterfly hadn't flapped its wings or had flapped in a different direction or with more or less force, the tornado may not have occurred in the same place or time, or at all.

Extreme Sensitivity to Initial Conditions

In 1961, the American meteorologist Edward Lorenz was working on some of the first computer simulations of weather and wanted to repeat the last steps of a previous simulation. Because computers at that time were slow and difficult to use, Lorenz tried to save time by using the intermediate output from a previous simulation as input for a new simulation. The printout, however, rounded the results to three numbers past the decimal point, and so he input "0.506" instead of entering the full "0.506127."

Lorenz assumed that this tiny difference in numbers would not significantly affect the results. To his surprise, the results of the second simulation were vastly different than the first, even though they should have been almost identical. The tiny difference in starting values produced completely different results. Lorenz's work emphasized how important sensitivity to initial conditions can be in real-world applications such as weather forecasting. In 1963, Lorenz published his findings for the New York Academy of Sciences and spoke at several scientific conferences. He quoted a colleague who said that if Lorenz's theory were correct, the flap of a seagull's wings could change the weather. He eventually changed this metaphor from a seagull's wings to a butterfly flap, and the butterfly effect was born.

A sensitivity to initial conditions is one of the defining characteristics of a complex system like the weather. I am no scientist, and realize that I am bastardizing the precise meaning of the mathematics a bit here, but I think that the butterfly effect can help us live better lives. Like the weather, human systems are complex, and people are sensitive to conditions. People's moods are affected by whether they slept well, the traffic, whether their pants feel loose or tight, a smile from the good-looking guy in the elevator, eBay auction results, and dozens of other small things. We can't predict what other people will do—even those we know very well—because there are many tiny variables that affect their thoughts and actions. Heck, most of us can't even predict how we will respond to tomorrow's challenges. We think we know how we will feel and act on Monday morning, but then a call from our mother-in-law on Sunday night changes everything. We might pass by a family having a picnic and feel the need to call our spouse and apologize for being a jerk earlier in the morning. If the children are being rambunctious, we might turn crankier. Political advertisements work because our opinions and beliefs are malleable and change when we learn new information. In Seattle, a front-runner for a City Council position lost her political race because she was arrested for driving while under the influence two weeks before Election Day—a butterfly flap that reverberated with a lot of folks, and not in a good way.

If the butterfly effect applies to human systems, the next logical question is to ask ourselves how we can use the big power of small things to improve our lives. This is not a straightforward process, however, because we cannot predict the outcomes. How do we influence what we can neither control nor forecast? Let's not forget, too, that each of us is a flapping butterfly. Even if we could control and predict our future behavior (which we can't—we can guess and we can form intentions, but who knows what's going to happen between now and then that will affect our choices), we have no way of knowing who else might be flapping in our direction.

TV news programs love tragic stories of butterfly flapping gone bad: road rage that caused a 12-car pileup and two fatalities; the childhood bullying that turned an otherwise smart kid into a killer; teenage curiosity about drugs that led to unprotected sex and then a pregnancy that altered the course of a girl's life and the lives of her grandchildren. Tiny decisions reverberate, and the reverberations reverberate, and then something happens. BAM, we weigh 300 pounds, and it seems like just yesterday we were frolicking in the surf in a yellow string bikini. Although the negative stories dominate the news and our memories, the butterfly effect can catalyze, and has catalyzed, wonderful outcomes—see the sidebar for a couple of true stories.

Wonderful Outcomes from the Butterfly Effect

I was giving a talk at the public library in Fayetteville, Georgia. Before the talk, I mingled with the group of about 20. I met a man who was starting a new business, but he had a hard time explaining what it was. Also in the group was a woman who was a freelance marketing communications writer (someone who makes a living explaining businesses). Another woman had brought pastries to the talk. People lined up for the pastries. The businessman and writer ended up next to each other in line, and they got to talking. POW, the man hired the writer to help explain his business. The head librarian flapped, I flapped, the businessman flapped, the writer flapped, and the woman who made the pastries flapped. All the flaps mattered. Had there been no pastries, the businessman and the writer might never have met.

Here's another example. A month before our wedding, I asked my fiancé Bill this question: If you could live anywhere, doing any kind of work, where would you live and what would you do? To my surprise, Bill said that he would like to live in Seattle and have his own geology consulting business. We lived in New Mexico at the time, and he had never mentioned Seattle or starting a business. I flapped a bit more and asked, well, what's keeping us from doing this? To make this long story short, I applied for a few jobs in Seattle, got an offer from a company that included full relocation benefits, and within six weeks we were living in Seattle and my husband had started his own consulting firm. We've now been living in Seattle for eight years, and Bill's company is thriving. Looking back to the day I asked the question, all I can do is shake my head and wonder. What would our lives be like if I had not asked this one question? I was just making conversation and was not trying to change the course of things.

The stories in the sidebar remind me of another fascinating aspect of the butterfly effect: We don't know which flaps will catalyze things the most. We act hundreds of times each day, and some of those actions will grow legs and reverberate more than others. Why? Because we are not the only ones flapping! We might go to a coffee shop on Monday and have a coffee. On Tuesday, we might go to the same coffee shop and meet our soul mate.

Actions lead to reactions—sometimes. We flap our butterfly wings and things happen that we cannot predict or control. If we looked back on our lives over the past five years, we might be able to piece together the small changes that affected the larger ones, but often we might have no idea. People we don't know and who don't know us are flapping today in directions that will change our circumstances next week.

Complex systems—they're fuzzy, enigmatic, and wonderful. And thus we can put the imperfect, unpredictable nature of humanity to work to improve our lives and the planet. The key to harnessing the power of the butterfly effect is that small, daily, directionally correct actions can change the world. Our goals define the futures we want to create. When our flaps are focused and frequent, our energies reverberate in a direction aligned with our goals; again, see the sidebar for an illustrative story.

It is much more powerful to act daily in small ways than to be a weekend warrior who does one or two big things each week. Remember, we don't know which butterfly flaps will reverberate to eventually catalyze a breakthrough. If you make only the occasional grand gesture, you will reduce the momentum and your chances for success. But if you devote 20 or 30 minutes of focused action each day, that may be all you need to achieve your goals.

All actions are not equal, and some will have a greater potential to produce reverberations. For example, let's imagine that you are thinking about starting your own business. There are hundreds of actions that you could take that would support this goal. You could do research online,

Getting That Book Written

A friend of mine wrote a children's book that shared a story about how to talk to children of foreign adoption about where they came from and why they are in a new country and with a new family. She and her husband adopted a son from Russia, and this book came from her experience. Her goal was to publish it and have all the book's proceeds benefit the Russian orphanage that took care of her son before she adopted him. When I found out about the book, the manuscript had been tucked away in a file folder for five years. She had told very few people about the project and was not sure how to proceed. She needed an illustrator and a publisher and advice about promotion. I shared her story with a few people at a book signing two days later at a Baltimore library. One of the library employees knew another library employee who illustrated children's books on the side. She and I connected our two friends, and BAM, my friend's book was plucked out from the dusty hallway closet and she had some momentum toward getting it completed. Just a couple flaps are all that are needed to generate progress.

apply for a business license, read books about successful entrepreneurs, meet with potential customers, and network with other small business owners. All these actions are directionally correct, and they all need to be done. However, those actions that connect two or more people, such as coffee shop networking, are better at gaining legs and reverberating to others who can make a difference to our lives.

Conversations are like invisible relay races. We love to talk about the conversations we have had. We tell our friends about what our others friends are up to, and we spread interesting news like butterflies flitting excitedly among nectar-rich flowers. We talk, and things change. And if we communicate well and repeatedly, things change quickly—the relay is on, and we have hundreds of flapping butterflies on our team. Conversations are the most potent types of butterfly flaps, especially when you share your goals and seek diverse input from others.

When we share our goals and intentions with others, they enroll in our vision and can double or triple our reach. You have heard of the self-fulfilling prophecy and the Pygmalion effect, right? Both these concepts theorize that expectations affect outcomes. If we have low expectations for our children or ourselves, we will likely get what we expect: low performance. But if we have high expectations, performance will be higher. We rise to the level of expectations. We see this belief being acted out at work, too. If your manager does not expect excellence, you and your teammates will not likely do your best work. Sharing our goals puts the power of the butterfly effect and the Pygmalion effect to work for our benefit. By sharing your goal to start a new business, you are reinforcing your intentions and the expectations you have for yourself. Each time you verbalize your goal, you hear and commit to it again. And you have friendly butterflies flapping on your behalf. Share your goal with two people each day for one week and you will see what I mean. This simple act—this small thing—has the power to shift your reality.

Remember the example in the sidebar above about Bill's goal to start his own business? That one conversation created a new reality. Sometimes it takes more than one conversation, and that's why we should share our goals with many people. You might even try helping your loved ones along by asking them about their goals. What if you asked your significant other the same question I asked Bill? If you could live anywhere, doing any kind of work, where would you live and what would you do? What might come from this conversation?

When we summon the courage to make requests that will help move our goals forward, our situation can change in an instant. Making requests allows us to shortcut the reverberation process and to move directly toward our preferred future. I think people hesitate to make requests because they don't want to seem selfish or impose on others. The types of requests that I'm suggesting are generally not the "give me" kind, although sometimes you should ask for what you want (you never know). I had a friend who wanted to make more than $100,000 and work only four days a week. She created a win-win proposal and made the request. And she got the job! The best "give me" requests offer win-win solutions that address a compelling need or opportunity.

Most of the time, request conversations should focus on gathering ideas, connections, accommodations, and coaching. Asking someone to spend 15 minutes with you so that you can pick her brain for ideas is a great way to enliven conversations about your goals. Sometimes we need to direct our requests to our significant others to ask for accommodations that will allow us to focus more time and uninterrupted energy on an important project. When was the last time you shared your goals with your significant other and asked him or her to help make your intentions a reality? Think about the last time you helped someone else. It felt great, didn't it? There are many caring people who would enjoy—and feel great about—helping you, too. Take the help!

While we are on the topic of goals, I think it is important to resist the urge to overdefine them. It is the nature of complex systems that the path forward will bring surprises and opportunities that we do not see today. If we define success too rigidly, we are more likely to overlook wonderful alternative paths. It is best when goals are inspiring and we are nimble. Like forecasts about weather systems, predictions about our lives get less accurate the further out they are.

Remember Lorenz's calculations given in the sidebar above? The tiniest of changes of the initial inputs—from 0.506127 to 0.506—resulted in two very different weather predictions. Each day is an initial input for our future. Sensitivity to initial conditions means that today's actions create tomorrow's sunshine and storms. During my day job as a business consultant, I work with leaders and businesses to help them improve results. I see many new systems touting their promise to increase success. I have been doing this work for 25 years, and yet I have seen nothing that comes close to the power of the butterfly effect. Sometimes the simplest answer is the best answer: Flap, flap, flap.

Turning Conversations into Results

My butterfly effect stories give you a feel for how you can take your goals and move them forward and how you can use pull coaching to turn conversations into results. As a coach, you can use catalytic techniques to help performers generate breakthroughs in results; here are five examples:

- Be it today.
- Go where the energy is.
- Make reverse requests.
- Provoke wild ideas.
- Invite a challenge.

Being It Today

I've coached many folks who had career growth goals—managers who wanted to be directors, directors who wanted to be VPs, and VPs who wanted to escape the rat race and start their own companies (like that's really escaping anything!). If you are coaching a performer who would like to get into a different job or role, talk with her about the power of "being it today." Being it today means acting in a way that is consistent with the new role, so that she and others will see her as a logical person for that role. Thus, if she is a manager who wants to be a director, she should act and think like a director. Doing this serves a couple of purposes:

- Decision makers will begin seeing her in the new role and see her as a good choice for the role when it opens up.
- If the performer has set a goal for the wrong reasons, or thinks she wants it but doesn't, this assignment will be revealing. For example, I have worked with people who wanted promotions for the money and title. But this is not a strong enough reason to go for a higher-level job, and walking a mile in shoes like those worn by the current incumbents will help the performer see this.

Here are several questions you can ask to help performers be it today:

- Who is a role model for what you are trying to do? How have they built their business, program, and/or team, and from which of these habits might you benefit if you adopted it today?
- What are you doing today that seems consistent with your goals, and how are your current habits inconsistent with the reality you want to create?

- Imagine that every person with whom you come in contact is the director of human resources and hiring manager for your dream position. How do you want to come across so that they see you in the role?
- Encourage performers to take on the persona that best fits their goals. As Gandhi once said, "Be the change you wish to see in the world." This also applies to personal development goals.

Going Where the Energy Is

I was talking with a communications and publicity manager recently and found myself using the phrase "go where the energy is" a few times. He noticed this phrase, and was struck by it. He suggested that it might make a nice story or book idea. We talked briefly about what going with the energy means and how I have applied this strategy in my life and work.

Part of being an optimistic, glass-is-half-full kind of person is experiencing disappointment. This may sound counterintuitive, but it is true. When we are optimistic, we believe that great things can and should happen. Sometimes they do, and sometimes they don't. Optimists feel disappointment more than pessimists do. Even so, I think that seeing the glass as half full is an advantage because it allows us to be ready and open for more possibilities. Being optimistic is also more pleasant for us and for those with whom we interact.

We can blindly move through the world hoping for the best, or we can be more targeted and improve our odds of being delighted. This is where going with the energy comes in. Going with the energy means noticing and approaching situations or people that are drawn to the situation or us. For example, when I did my motorcycle book tour around the country a few years ago, I went to the towns where my most active and interested blog and book readers lived. As a result, I did not go to Los Angeles, San Francisco, or New York, the top three places most authors visit on book tours. I went where the energy was, not where it was not.

This practice of going with the energy also helps me focus my efforts as a consultant. I talk with many people, and it is my job to offer and sell consulting services. If I treated every lead and every prospect the same way, I would be chasing many cold avenues, suffering from more disappointment, and enjoying less success. But when I go where the energy is, I can create a strong partnership with clients and deliver the services they seek. It is a win-win.

And this same strategy can apply to all kinds of professionals. How often do we ram through projects or decisions or feel as if we must bribe people to attend meetings or training sessions? Go where the energy is, not where it is not. I was a director of organization development many years back, and I remember offering a set of services to the department leaders. A few came to me immediately and asked for help and support, and we did great work together. I did not waste my energy on the departments that would only engage in these services if they were forced to or told it was mandatory. Ditto with my coaching services. Like Marshall Goldsmith, I do not waste my time coaching the uncoachable—those performers who do not want to be coached and who have closed themselves to learning.

Author's Aside

Marshall Goldsmith is famous for saying he won't coach the uncoachable. Check out his sassy but wonderful opinions on his website, at www .marshallgoldsmith.com.

How can you use the strategy of going with the energy in your work and life? Don't waste time, energy, and positivity by chasing after people or projects that are running in the opposite direction. Take note of the people who are drawn to your work or messages—and see and respond to those who are enrolled in your projects or passions. Be grateful for the energy that people share with you and on your behalf. As a performer, pull coaching from those who seem interested in your goals. And as a coach, seek performers who are pulling your coaching in and seem eager to learn from you.

Making Reverse Requests

I am a fan of making requests to generate breakthroughs. If we do not ask, how will the people who care about us know what we need? Well, here's a different twist on how to use the power of a request—I call it the reverse request.

A reverse request happens when you help others make requests. Here are a few examples of reverse requests:

- You know what someone wants, and so you go ahead and offer it (or some version of it), sparing her the difficult task of asking for it.
- You engage in a conversation that helps someone articulate what she wants. Then you ask what you or someone else could do that would be most helpful.
- You provide the courage—courage on loan—that helps someone else make something big happen.

I have a friend who is very conservative when it comes to being assertive about her hopes, dreams, and wishes. She does not want to be a bother, and so she feels a bit selfish asking about these things closest to her heart (I am not putting words in her mouth; we have talked about this). But it's not selfish to make requests, because when we are at our best, everyone wins. Yet because this is a struggle for my friend, she generally does not get around to sharing her requests. Sometimes I put myself in her shoes and share with her what I think she would ask for if she had the courage. So far, I have been right every time. When I offer her help, she says "yes," and things surge forward for her. I would bet that you have a friend or coworker like this, too.

Earlier in the chapter, I shared the story of how my husband Bill and I came to move from New Mexico to Seattle. This ended up being a reverse request. Once I learned that his goal was to open a geology consulting firm in Seattle, I made the request that he had not made when I said "Well, why wouldn't we just do that?"

This reverse request helped to catalyze our focused actions, and we ended up in Seattle just a few weeks after our conversation about it began. *Pow!* Would we have moved to Seattle one day anyway? Who knows. Did it happen much more quickly because of the reverse request? Absolutely. Here's the point: Bill had had it in his head, probably for years, that he would like to live and work in Seattle. Your friends and coworkers have dreams too, and I bet some would surprise you.

Reverse requests are a great way to help catalyze breakthroughs. And they're fun! Be a "yes" person, someone who helps performers see what's possible, even in the face of great challenges or situations that seem impossible. If you take the time and care to proactively advocate for someone else (offer help, loan her your courage), you may demolish a major barrier standing in her way.

Provoking Wild Ideas

Do you work with performers who have a tough time thinking outside the box? The good news is that you don't have to be outside the box to catalyze a performer's creativity. A performer will be more creative if she considers wild ideas. Some of my most memorable breakthroughs have resulted from a wild idea, and many of these ideas have come from helpful coaching conversations.

So what's a "wild idea"? It's a thought or question that is a little strange, unreasonable, or counterintuitive. Provoking wild ideas is an easy coaching technique that involves asking great questions or giving prompts like these:

- Think about the ideas that you have come up with over the last month. Did you dismiss any wild ideas?
- Think of a partnership that would be just too good to be true.
- Think of a sponsor that you think would be a long shot.
- Who, in your wildest dreams, would you like to hear pitching or telling other people about you?
- If you could have any job or contract project, what would it be?

- If you were feeling *really brave* and confident, what requests would you make?
- What dream or goal have you been keeping to yourself?

You never know what question will catalyze a breakthrough for the performer, so you should talk often about wild ideas. And these wild ideas might also evoke more traditional ideas or help the performer reconnect with her purpose or work.

Inviting a Challenge

I am a big fan of welcoming naysayers and devil's advocates into the conversation. Not only is this a great way to unearth diverse ideas, it also helps enroll people in the process and improve their acceptance of my work. Naysayers make great evangelists!

Inviting a challenge means asking others to critique our work—to really critique it. This may not be the easiest idea to sell to another performer, and you don't really want to sell it, per se. If the performer is coachable—highly coachable—she might be ready to invite a challenge. Give it a try yourself, and then you will have a story you can share with other performers. Say "Bring it on!"

Author's Aside

As a writer, I often will send a chapter out to several colleagues and ask them to rip it apart—no sugarcoating. As a matter of fact, I did this with the introduction to this book. When I tell training participants about this technique, I can see that many are a bit uncomfortable with the level of vulnerability we show when asking for a tough critique. I can also see that they are very interested and intrigued, perhaps wondering what the odds are that this technique will blow up in their faces. But no guts, no glory!

Take on this mantra of inviting challenges for a month, and see how it affects your focus and results. I like to designate a devil's advocate at team meetings to encourage diverse ideas and spice up the conversation. Rotate the responsibility to give everyone practice. Here's an example of how to invite a challenge for a new idea you are thinking of proposing:

- Create a rough draft of your proposal. Offer the rationale, describe the idea, and give as much context as possible.
- Select a small group of pre–early adopters. These should be people who you think can—and will—give you interesting feedback. Include the people who are the most logical detractors.
- Create a list of questions you would like your pre–early adopters to answer. Include questions like "What are all the reasons that you think this idea will not work?" and "What about this idea do you find least appealing?"
- Invite the pre–early adopters to review the plan and provide feedback. If possible, invite them to a 15-minute meeting where you hand out the rough plan and questions, and ask for their feedback within a certain number of days. If a meeting is not possible or practical, give each person a quick call asking them to participate and letting them know they will soon get an email with the plan and questions attached. Let your pre–early adopters know that you do not want them to sugarcoat the feedback and that you believe that all feedback is a gift—even when it is tough to hear.
- Once you get the feedback, thank the pre–early adopters sincerely and warmly, regardless of how critical they were of your ideas. Then use their feedback to improve your plan.

You will find that when you invite a challenge, you create many more fans than detractors. Even those who do not like the idea will become more accepting of the revised plan's implementation. It's magic! In addition, when you establish an environment in which people feel comfortable sharing their concerns and ideas, you will be more likely to hear about and catch mistakes and head off problems as they emerge. And you do want to know what's happening as soon as possible; otherwise, your options for dealing with barriers will quickly diminish.

Inviting a challenge can be a wonderful and enjoyable experience when performers keep their egos from getting in the way. As a coach, model the way and share your successes with the practice of inviting a challenge, and you may just help a performer reach a higher level of success and peer acceptance.

Summing Up

These breakthrough techniques use the big power of small actions. My experiences as a coach have been richer since I started experimenting with how to catalyze breakthroughs. I use these techniques to help myself and—when invited—love to share them with others.

In the next chapter, we'll consider several important ways to create a work environment where coaching up and down the generations can prosper.

Chapter 6

Cultivating a Coachable and Coaching Environment for All Generations

Considerations for Senior Leaders and Trainers

I was speaking at an ASTD International Conference about my book *Hip and Sage: Staying Smart, Cool and Competitive in the Workplace* (Haneberg 2009). During the after-talk chitchat, I asked several training professionals how well their development offerings encouraged the mixing and mingling of younger and older workers. The blank looks on their faces were telling—this was not something they had thought about before. I have heard and seen similar responses from many of my readers and clients. In fact, I know of very few organizations that are taking proactive steps to create a multigenerational learning environment. (Here I am focusing on generations, but the same learning strategies can help build relationships among performers with diverse backgrounds, ethnicity, experience levels, and other varying characteristics.)

And yet—and yet this might be the single most effective thing an organization can do to ensure that coaching, learning, and collaboration are done up and down the generations. Leaders, human resources (HR) and organization development professionals, and trainers—the folks who establish learning strategies and shape the learning culture—are in the best position to lead the charge for multigenerational relationship building.

This is the key lever: relationship building. We know that there is little difference in what the performers of each generation want from coaches. They want to own their learning, they want coaching when they are ready, and they don't want coaches to take over or dance around their input. What's getting in the way is exposure and familiarity—a lack of relationship and mutual respect. When performers get to know one another, they learn what they have in common, and they begin to see past their flawed first impressions of each other. Alas, the mixing of the generations often does not naturally happen. Many kinds of barriers can get in the way of multigenerational relationship building:

- Differing use of and comfort with technology, and thereby different ways performers meet and gather.
- Differing looks, manners, and habits and opinions about these choices.
- Differing preferences for work hours and flexibility.
- Age and organization level are often positively correlated, which results in a natural separation of the generations.
- Differing hobbies and personal interests, which affect who people sit with in the lunchroom.
- Our seemingly endless media blabber about the four generations, which reinforces their differences rather than their areas of commonality.

If organizations do not make a concerted effort to create a learning and working environment that builds multigenerational relationships, what are the chances that this will happen on its own? The good news is that organizations can implement several small changes that will significantly improve the level and quality of conversations that occur up and down the generations. I recommend learning strategies that fall into these three buckets:

- Ways to bring people together in formal settings.
- Ways to encourage informal gatherings of diverse individuals.
- Ways to improve the quality of conversations in all work gatherings.

Take a few moments to assess your current learning strategies, structures, and resources in relation to the following suggestions.

Bringing People Together in Formal Settings

Every development event (training classes, communication meetings, retreats, brown bag lunches, and so on) offers the opportunity to build multigenerational relationships. I would assume that your training sessions are accomplishing this goal to some degree already (training classes often bring together people who do not work together on a daily basis). Consider these ideas to increase the frequency and quality of relationship building up and down the generations:

- Mix up the seating chart. Do you let people sit wherever they like? Take a few minutes to create seating assignments that mix people by generation and department.
- Rotate learning group leadership. Do you let the natural leader emerge and become the spokesperson for group activities and report-outs? Rotate the assignment so that every table mate gets a chance to play the leadership role. Doing this will help balance participation and help people get to know each other.
- Offer training sessions that will appeal to a mix of people, like "How to Use New Technologies for Project Management." Recruit project managers of all ages to attend and share their experiences.
- Utilize team-building exercises that show off every performer's talents to build interest and mutual respect.
- Recruit unconventional training leaders to reduce preconceived notions about how talent is distributed among the generations. Ask a Baby Boomer to help lead a social networking media brown bag, and ask a Millennial to lead a session about creative ways to encourage knowledge transfer from more to less experienced workers.
- Use new technologies and communication tools during training sessions to increase your organization's overall familiarity with

these innovations and to reduce unfamiliarity with them as a barrier to relationship building.

- If you use webinars or offer virtual learning tools, add phone breakout sessions to each class and assign pairs of diverse people to talk with each other by phone to complete learning assignments.

Trainers should take the initiative to think of ways to increase relationship building before every class. You have people in a room—captive—so don't waste the opportunity to nudge them into getting to know each other. It's good for them!

Encouraging Informal Learning Opportunities

At her keynote speech during the 2009 ASTD International Conference, Cisco Systems' chief learning officer, Karie Willyard, said that 78 percent of all learning is informal. This is a high number! Each workplace will be different, but I think it would be safe to assume that the majority of the learning that is occurring within your workplace is informal. Examples of informal learning include

- Ad hoc conversations—in person, on the phone, and online.
- Written, audio, and video content—in person, on the phone, and online. This includes bulletin boards, newsletters, weblogs, social networks (which combine content and conversations), and business books.
- The learning that occurs on the job, during projects and when collaborating with colleagues.

If informal learning constitutes more than half the learning where you work, how much time do you spend creating and implementing informal learning strategies? I would encourage HR and training departments to dedicate at least half their time, financial resources, and attention to making informal learning more fruitful and effective. Part of your efforts should be to capitalize on opportunities to make information learning environments fertile ground for multigenerational relationship building. Here are a few ideas to get you started:

- Create an internal learning weblog, and invite performers from all generations to guest post on topics of interest.
- Facilitate team meetings on occasion, and include team-building activities—without them even knowing you have done this. (This is a technique I call stealth training—giving people training when they don't know it. I love this as a tool because it can have an impact and help develop a stronger informal learning culture. They know the meeting was doubly fruitful, but might not know why!)
- Use bulletin boards and newsletters to offer information about how to use new technologies for communication and team projects.
- Record podcasts and videocasts with performers from all generations and at all experience levels.
- Keep a library of great resources available, and encourage teams to bring two or three new books or DVDs to each team meeting to offer for checking out. (I'm sorry, but most learning libraries I have seen have been lame. Get the good stuff, and take an active role in exposing people to the resources.)
- Create cheat sheets for great one-to-ones, coaching conversations, ways to improve team meetings, and other topics that performers could quickly reference and use.
- Organize learning salons (informal discussions without an assigned leader). Salons are organic, stimulating, and transformative because they can jump-start conversations that will have sufficient energy behind them to later lead to action. Comments that flow at such "salon-style" discussions become catalysts for changing how people approach their work. I love salons.

The possibilities are endless and exciting! I have been an internal leader in many departments—including human resources, organization development, and training—and I have seen the value that having a robust information learning environment brings to the team. All these ideas engage people and create more areas of common ground and understanding.

Improving the Quality of Conversations in All Work Gatherings

Getting people together is a waste of time if they do not communicate well during the meeting. Leaders and development professionals can and should implement strategies and practices that improve the quality of work conversations. The more effectively people converse, the deeper their relationships will become. And the deeper their relationships, the more robust their partnerships will be—and you will thus see more and better coaching up and down the generations.

● ● ●

conversations = relationships = coaching = success

● ● ●

For this reason, I see facilitating great meetings as time well spent—even for upper-level HR and training managers and leaders. Yes, I am suggesting that the director of training or director of HR should offer to facilitate meetings. I can think of no higher-return activity than helping a group of smart people do their best work together. When you facilitate meetings, do so with an eye toward building the team's capacity for great dialogue. Here are three of my facilitation goals: to create provocation, evocation, and a deep versus wide focus.

Provocation

Learning often occurs as a result of dissonance—some difference between what we thought was true and another perspective. When conversations are provocative, they challenge performers to think in new ways. We should not try to be provocative just to be provocative, however. We need to notice where performers are getting stuck, then offer questions or ideas that nudge them forward. Something is provocative when it causes a strong reaction. For example, all these emotions might be caused by provocation: annoyance, anger, excitement, fascination, curiosity, or a feeling of invitation. We don't want to routinely anger performers, but an occasional bit of anger or frustration, followed by a good, deep conversation, can be a great learning enhancer.

Evocation

When we are evocative, we help others see things from their own perspective—we put performers in the scene for themselves. Evocative learning is very connecting. When performers think about a concept or apply it to their situation, they are being evoked. Great conversations provoke evocation. We want performers to imagine how they will apply the concepts or techniques in their own departments.

Deep versus Wide

It is best to address fewer topics and spend more time on each one. One-hour staff meetings with 15 agenda items drive me crazy and are usually a waste of time. The deeper you can get into a topic, the deeper will be your learning and relationship building. Help groups take the time needed to hear many perspectives, and ask great questions so that all the performers can make a connection between the topic and their work and realize its relevance.

Summing Up

Are the conversations happening in your workplace provocative, evocative, and deep? Are your informal and formal development opportunities facilitating relationship building up and down the generations? For your next management staff meeting, share this chapter—ask those attending to read it before the meeting—and start a conversation about how you can catalyze multigenerational collaboration and coaching.

Conclusion

Into the Future We Go

When we connect with people, we relate based on common needs, goals, interests, or experiences. You and your best friends and family members have many areas of connection, as would longtime co-workers or two new employees hired on the same day and coming from the same engineering school. Two professionals from different functions, with different backgrounds, who are 40 years apart in age, have fewer obvious connections. But just because the connections are not obvious does not mean they do not exist.

Coaching up and down the generations is a vision for connections that are formed in spite of significant differences. Catalytic coaches and engaged performers actively seek conversations with professionals of all ages and experience levels, and they quickly uncover common points of interest. Like the wood rafters under your house's roof, each connection strengthens the relationship. Be the one to uncover and discover common interests, values, pet peeves, and goals.

This may not have been the book you were expecting, but I hope it becomes the one you use to help you and those with whom you work become more successful as coaches and performers. Like a good business book, coaching conversations are best when they are helpful but not too prescriptive. I remember hearing Meg Wheatley speak at a conference several years ago. (She wrote a great book, *Leadership and the New Science;* see Wheatley 2001.) She shared a story about a company that had improved its retention and results by adopting a new structure and organizational model. During the Q&A portion of her talk, an audience member asked her if she would recommend that the same approach be implemented in companies like hers. Wheatley said, "no," which surprised the audience. She went on to say that it would be foolish to think that a solution that worked at Company A would work at Company B. Company B deserves its own solution.

No two organizations are alike—cultures are different, histories are different, and goals are different. Solutions are also products of their time— the same solution implemented at the same organization at two different times will produce different results (going back to sensitivity of conditions and chaos theory). The reason that I share this example from Wheatley's speech is that I think she was right, and this is why I now write books that are less prescriptive and more catalytic—or at least my aim is that they are catalytic, and I hope this one has been for you.

I invite you to experiment with this belief as a coach, too. Each performer deserves her own solution, and she needs to be the one to select it, embrace it, and implement it. As catalysts, we build a bridge, light the path, and give her our hand to help her demolish or jump over obstacles. Coaching is amazing work and a privilege.

Our workplaces need great coaches more than ever to help bring together the four generations and the dozens of other various characteristics that can keep us apart when our relationships remain on the surface. The surface is where these differences matter—the green hair, the old-timey bow tie, the Buick, and the Crotch Rocket (a fast street motorcycle). But when our relationships deepen, we meet the real people beneath the packaging—the caring, smart, and committed professionals who have been there all along.

References

Barry, Dave. 1990. *Dave Barry Turns 40.* New York: Fawcett/Ballantine.

Coupland, Douglas. 1991. *Generation X: Tales for an Accelerated Culture.* New York: Macmillan.

Ferrazzi, Keith, with Tahl Raz. 2005. *Never Eat Alone.* Published by the author; see www.keithferrazzi.com.

Ford, Jeffrey, and Laurie Ford. 2009. *The Four Conversations: Daily Communication That Gets Results.* San Francisco: Berrett-Koehler.

Haneberg, Lisa. 2007. *Two Weeks to a Breakthrough: How to Zoom toward Your Goal in 14 Days or Less.* San Francisco: Jossey-Bass.

———. 2009. *Hip and Sage: Staying Smart, Cool and Competitive in the Workplace.* Boston: Davies-Black; Arlington, VA: ASTD Press.

McLuhan, Marshall. 1951/2002. *The Mechanical Bride: Folklore of Industrial Man.* Berkeley, CA: Gingko Press. (Orig. pub. 1951.)

———. 1962. *The Gutenberg Galaxy: The Making of Typographic Man.* Toronto: University of Toronto Press.

———. 1964/1994. *Understanding Media: The Extensions of Man.* Cambridge, MA: MIT Press. (Orig. pub. 1964.)

Rogers, Carl. 1995. *On Becoming a Person: A Therapist's View of Psychotherapy.* Orlando: Houghton Mifflin Harcourt. (Orig. pub. 1961.)

Wheatley, Margaret J. 2001. *Leadership and the New Science: Discovering Order in a Chaotic World.* San Francisco: Berrett-Koehler.

About the Author

Lisa Haneberg is nonfiction writer, speaker, and consultant with 25 years of experience in the areas of management, leadership, and personal and organizational success. She is the vice president and organization development practice lead for MPI Consulting, a boutique consulting firm headquartered in Cincinnati. She consults in the areas of organization development, management and leadership training, and human resources and has worked for and with several *Fortune* 500 companies, including Black & Decker, Intel, Mead Paper, and Amazon.com. She has written 10 books and numerous articles and essays, and she is the author of the popular management blog Management Craft (www .managementcraft.com). She lives with her husband, two big dogs, and two cats in Cincinnati. She enjoys travel, reading, writing, and driving her purple motorcycle named Hazel down winding roads. Feel free to contact her through her website at www.lisahaneberg.com.

Other books by Lisa Haneberg:

Organization Development Basics (ASTD Press, 2005)
More Space (contributing author; Astronaut, 2005)
Coaching Basics (ASTD Press, 2006)
Focus Like a Laser Beam: 10 Ways to Do What Matters Most (Jossey-Bass, 2006)
Two Weeks to a Breakthrough: How to Zoom toward Your Goal in 14 Days or Less (Jossey-Bass, 2007)
10 Steps to Be a Successful Manager (ASTD Press, 2007)
Developing Great Managers: 20 Power Hours (ASTD Press, 2008)

Hip and Sage: Staying Smart, Cool and Competitive in the Workplace (Davies-Black / ASTD Press, 2009)

High-Impact Middle Management: Solutions for Today's Busy Public-Sector Managers (ASTD Press, 2010)

The High-Impact Middle Manager: Powerful Strategies to Thrive in the Middle (ASTD Press, 2010)

About Berrett-Koehler Publishers

Berrett-Koehler is an independent publisher dedicated to an ambitious mission: Creating a World That Works for All.

We believe that to truly create a better world, action is needed at all levels—individual, organizational, and societal. At the individual level, our publications help people align their lives with their values and with their aspirations for a better world. At the organizational level, our publications promote progressive leadership and management practices, socially responsible approaches to business, and humane and effective organizations. At the societal level, our publications advance social and economic justice, shared prosperity, sustainability, and new solutions to national and global issues.

Visit our website

Go to www.bkconnection.com to read exclusive excerpts of new books, get special discounts, see videos of our authors, read their blogs, find out about author appearances and other BK events, browse our complete catalog, and more!

Get the *BK Communiqué,* our free eNewsletter

News about Berrett-Koehler, yes—new book announcements, special offers, author interviews. But also news by Berrett-Koehler authors, employees, and fellow travelers. Tales of the book trade. Links to our favorite websites and videos—informative, amusing, sometimes inexplicable. Trivia questions—win a free book! Letters to the editor. And much more!

See a sample issue: www.bkconnection.com/BKCommunique.

BK° Berrett–Koehler Publishers, Inc.
San Francisco. *www.bkconnection.com*

Index

Note: *f* represents a figure and *t* represents a table.